The Making of
the American Citizenry

Chandler Publications
in Political Science
Victor Jones, Editor

THE MAKING OF
THE AMERICAN CITIZENRY

An Introduction to Political Socialization

MICHAEL P. RICCARDS
State University of New York
College at Buffalo

CHANDLER PUBLISHING COMPANY
An Intext Publisher
New York and London

Copyright © 1973 by Intext Press, Inc.

All rights reserved. No part of this book may be reprinted, reproduced, or utilized in any form or by any electronic, mechanical, or other means, now known or hereafter invented, including photocopying and recording, or in any information storage and retrieval system, without permission in writing from the Publisher.

Library of Congress Cataloging in Publication Data

Riccards, Michael P
    The making of the American citizenry.

    (Chandler publications in political science)
    Bibliography: p.
    1. Political socialization.   2. Child study.
3. United States—Social conditions—1960–
I. Title.
JA76.R52   301.5'92   73–1678
ISBN 0–8102–0471–1

Intext Educational Publishers
257 Park Avenue South
New York, New York 10010

Contents

Preface ix

Introduction 1

1 Political Socialization: Concept and Process 5

The Extent of Socialization 5
The Importance of Being American 8
The American as Citizen 9
The History of Political Socialization 11
The Typology 16
Summary 19

2 The Stirrings of Moral Authority 23

Imitation 24
Trust and Efficacy 25
Concepts of Rules 26
Making Moral Judgments 28
Summary 31

3   The Family as Predisposition   35

    The Problems of Predisposition   36
    Political Guilt   37
    Partisan Affiliation   40
    The Family Power Structure   40
    Maternal Influence   43
    Recruitment   46
    Transmitting Issue Attitudes   47
    Summary   48

4   The Social Nexus: Sex, Class, Peers, and Ethnicity   53

    Sex Differences   53
    The Consequences of Class   56
    Peer Groups   58
    The Ethnic Factor   61
    Summary   64

5   The Child's Political Community   69

    The Benevolent State   69
    The Young Citizen   73
    Abstract Allegiance   74
    Places Elsewhere   76
    Summary   81

6   The Role of the School   85

    Creating Loyalty   86
    The Textbook Democracy   87
    The Teacher's Influence   89
    Civic Awareness   92
    Passive and Active Participation   93

Intelligence Differences   95
Summary   96

7   An Overview of Adult Socialization   101

Preparatory Leadership   103
College Dissent   104
Generational Leadership   107
Retrospective Leadership   107
Fitting Together   109
Attitude Change   110
Summary   111

8   A Note on Methodology   115

Surveying Children   115
Differences in Development   116
Attitudes and Nonattitudes   117
Summary   119

Bibliographical Essay   121

Index   127

TO BARBARA

Dal primo giorno ch' i' vidi il suo viso
In questa vita, infino a questa vista,
Non m' è il seguire al mio cantar preciso.

Preface

This study synthesizes and interprets the vastly growing literature on political socialization. In the process, it draws upon the research not only of political scientists, but also of psychologists, educators, and sociologists. No study can do justice to the subtlety and scope of all of these scholars, but it is my hope that this work will serve more as a stimulus than as a deterrent to further exploration.

Over the years, political socialization has been examined by many different scholars from a variety of viewpoints. Psychologists have generally emphasized the important relationships between human development and political behavior, while many sociologists and political scientists have called attention to the systemic effects of socialization. And, of course, philosophers and educators have for centuries concerned themselves with the beliefs and attitudes that are inculcated in the young. The very title of this book is an attempt to acknowledge the continuity of interest in this subject. One of the first modern social scientists to examine political socialization was Charles Merriam, who entitled his study *The Making of Citizens*.

In addition to the insights I have garnered from older studies, I am also indebted to many of my colleagues for their assistance, especially Philip Abbott, David Cortland Brown, Jerome Kraus, and Howard Park. Larry Kerpelman, Roberta Sigel, Pauline M. Vaillancourt, and John Wahlke each made available some important unpublished work, which is cited in the following chapters. Fred Greenstein, Bertram Raven, and Raymond Stone were kind enough to make suggestions and comments on the original manuscript, and I have greatly benefitted from their wisdom. Lastly, much more than my thanks goes to my wife, Barbara, to whom this book is dedicated.

The Making of
the American Citizenry

Introduction

Let us be candid—there is no general theory of personality and this deficiency must influence anyone's ability to comprehend political behavior. However, because of the many empirical studies that have been done, we can do more than speculate aimlessly about what people know and believe. Certainly, for example, we have a more sophisticated understanding of voting behavior than social scientists and historians had a generation or two ago.

It is logical then that in the process of trying to understand political behavior scholars should seek to explain how people acquire certain predispositions toward the political world. A considerable amount of time has been spent on examining children, not because scholars were interested in what children believe per se, but because they assumed that the "child is father to the man."

In the last decade or so many political scientists have expressed an interest in the process of civic inculcation, a process which they term *political socialization*. This book examines the field of political socialization from two varied but related perspectives. The first perspective explores the ways in which political attitudes and values are transmitted by the main agents of socialization and how these attitudes and values are affected by certain social variables. This is essentially the standard treatment of the field and much of the current research deals with these problems.

The second perspective is based on the view that political socialization is part of the broader patterns of human development that follow a fairly regular sequence of stages throughout the life cycle. However, there is one complication: politics is a symbolic realm and people must develop a sensibility toward its forms. When we look at civic socialization, we are really trying to describe the development of this political sensibility over time.

In some societies the political sensibility is highly developed, while in others it is almost nonexistent. One may argue that in a participant culture this sensibility is accentuated. This statement is undoubtedly true. In our society at this time we can see how certain stages in human maturation go along with certain stages of political development. The complexities of this viewpoint will be examined later.

The first chapter deals with the concept of political socialization and why we, as a nation, have been so concerned with it. This chapter also presents a developmental framework in which each stage and its characteristics are identified.

The second chapter examines the early predispositions which a child develops on questions of trust, self-esteem, efficacy, and morality. The influence of Jean Piaget on child psychology has been immense and his findings are discussed in this chapter.

The third chapter covers the role of the family in the political socialization process. While we are all aware of the family's great influence in child development, the exact parameters of that influence are often rather blurred. This chapter seeks to define some of these parameters.

The fourth chapter summarizes what little we know about the effects that sex role, peer group, race, and ethnic background have on the socialization process.

The fifth chapter discusses the child's concepts of community and authority and how these concepts change over time. The findings of the major socialization studies are presented and incorporated into the developmental framework.

The sixth chapter examines the role of the school in the political socialization process. Emphasis is placed on the effects of differential socialization from a variety of perspectives.

The seventh chapter carries the socialization process into adulthood and old age. It does not summarize the findings on political behavior, but it simply identifies and explains in a brief way the final three stages of development.

The last chapter is a critique of the methodology and assumptions that characterize present-day political socialization research. Hopefully, after finishing it the reader will not wonder why he decided to plow through the other chapters in the first place.

It must be remembered that the systematic study of political socialization is a relatively new field. While the major outlines of that field are sketched out in the following pages, some of the evidence presented may seem unclear or even contradictory with what has been said in other studies. In addition, there are research areas such as ethnicity, peer groups, the role of the media, and adult socialization where the findings are meager. Yet even with all of these difficulties, political socialization, using different methods and with a different vocabulary, has returned to one of the basic concerns of civilized man. It has made us conscious once again of the web of social relationships which influences even the most solitary individual. We soon come to realize that we are studying not just others but ourselves as well.

one

Political Socialization
Concept and Process

To speak of man outside of society is to put forth a contradiction in terms. As the first great empirical political scientist, Aristotle, noted, one who lives outside society is either a beast or a god, for surely he cannot be termed a man. Indeed, the strange tales we have, both apocryphal and true, of wolf children indicate that humans once they reach a certain minimum age, can function biologically without the companionship of other people. Yet they are like animals: devoid of arts and letters, unable to communicate on more than the most rudimentary of levels, and barely able to cope with changes in their natural environment.[1] Because of a prolonged period of maturation which exceeds that of any other species, the human infant is dependent on the attention and care of adult society for a considerable time. Thus from the beginning of his life man becomes socialized, and in the process he is continually involved in a rather complicated set of learning experiences. In general, then, we may define socialization as the *internalization of the norms and characteristic life style of the social environment in which one lives.*[2]

The Extent of Socialization

It is important to realize that as any society becomes larger and more interrelated, the possibilities of conflict increase substantially. One of the main functions of the socialization process is to channel, direct, or repress those kinds of behavior that are deemed antisocial, dangerous, or even deviant. In this way the cohesiveness of the society is maintained in spite of considerable stress. Because of the importance that the socialization process has for the system and its effect on molding the individual, many times we do not fully comprehend the pervasiveness of that process in our own lives.

In actuality, the range of human potentialities and life styles is extraordinarily broad. Our ability to do, to think, or even to imagine is far greater than any one person or even any one society can envision. But in the process of trying to establish cohesive social units, the laws, rules, norms, and customs of a community promote or proscribe certain activities and thought patterns. Society is then both a source of bondage and a wellspring of freedom. The inevitable tension between the individual and society has been one of the central themes of Western philosophy and psychology. This tension arises from man's continual realization that civilization is both liberating and stifling. For our culture, our artifacts, and our social order we pay a price: the repression of some natural instincts and, more importantly, the foreclosing of certain avenues of possibilities before they are even considered.[3] It is for this reason that every man is partly an outlaw in his own society. He feels, thinks, and dreams things that he knows he should not. As Shakespeare's Caesar recognized, the most dangerous men in a state are those who think too much.

For most of us, however, socialization is so effective that we are unaware that our conventions are just one choice from among many. We do not realize that our paradigm of society is partly a product of our tacit assumptions. To take one example, for generations and even millenia the political, social, and ethical systems of mankind have been based on one primary assumption—scarcity. The basic task of mankind has always been survival—survival in the face of staggering odds. To overcome this, men have subordinated their creative, erotic, and intellectual energies to forestall the consequences of economic scarcity. But long after scarcity ceases to be an economic problem, it will remain a philosophical and political one. The question then will be how to create artificial scarcity so that our social systems can work just as before.[4]

Those who point up that any social system, however successful, is only one possible paradigm are seen as radicals. The reason for this is that the first step in discrediting the old order is to put forth the notion that things do not necessarily have to be the way they are.[5] But even if one does realize that all societies are based on convention, it is impossible not to be influenced by the magnitude of that convention. The social order is a part of us; its mark is almost as firmly and deeply implanted as the most basic of our psychological needs. Indeed, few people really comprehend how fully they are socialized—even in their modes of expressing opposition to that very process.

Socialization, then, is highly effective in integrating individuals into the community and in maintaining the social system with a minimum of conflict. It is for this reason that socialization is seen more often as the handing down of truth itself than simply as the inculcation of the predominant social values.

Functionally, the process of socialization also helps to create roles into which new members of society can easily fit. Indeed, we relate to people—even those we are intimate with—in terms of role. Mother, father, lover, child, friend, student, doctor, and mechanic are all roles and each is linked to a specific network of expectations which is associated with it.

In our relations with strangers, we react in the same way. When we meet a new acquaintance, we first ask his name (his historical background) and soon after his occupation (his social function). The importance of role and function carries over from interpersonal relations to politics as well. One example of this is our view of the Presidency. The American people have historically expressed confidence in the Chief Executive not because they have examined the specific individual to see if he is personally trustworthy, but because trust is (or has been) one of the expectations of the office or role.[6]

Socialization, however, is much more than the mere acquisition of a person's role and function. It is the very process whereby man learns his culture and is made human in the sense that we know the term. Of course, all forms of animal life engage in some sort of learning. The most basic type of learning is situational, where the organism adopts or alters a behavioral response because of some experience. This sort of adaptation is necessary to survival. The second type of learning is when an organism acquires this sort of adaptive response and makes it part of its routine behavior; such adaptation is termed social learning. However, the most interesting and unique kind of learning is done by man alone. This type of learning is characterized by the development, aggregation, and manipulation of symbolic forms and representations.[7] It is at this stage that knowledge is codified and passed on; the foundations of culture itself are laid down.

The central importance of human socialization is that it provides access or entry to this world of symbolic learning of which politics is one part. Like art, science, and religion, politics is a creative act. It is little wonder that Aristotle, a man not usually given to hyperbole, called the founder of the first state the greatest of benefactors. One might also add that such a man was the greatest of dreamers as well.

Generally we tend to think of politics in terms of its processes: conflict resolution, resource allocation, coalition formation. Yet it must be obvious that this view is too narrow and incomplete. A more comprehensive definition of politics must also include the notion that it is *a state of fluctuating self-awareness about those things that are important to the community as a whole.* Such an awareness is heavily laden with symbolic formulations of authority, legitimacy, community, transcendence, and survival, which are all components of the basic myth structure of any polity.[8] Such formulations must be passed on, or socialized, if a political system is to endure for any considerable period of time.

The Importance of Being American

The process of passing on these formulations is termed *political socialization*. More specifically, political socialization may be defined as *the inculcation in the uninitiated of those attitudes, beliefs, and values which explain the political world*. All political systems have some sort of political socialization process and the United States is no exception. Indeed, few countries have been as conscious of the need for "civic education" as the United States.

There are many reasons for this awareness, but the most important of all is that in a rather short period of time the United States has had to assimilate over 35 million immigrants, many of them possessing few of the original Anglo-American presuppositions about government. The results of this massive acculturation are too huge to catalogue fully, but among them are tremendous cultural shock for immigrants, the rise of urban ghettos, the denigration of European customs and traditions, and the great ambivalence of second-generation Americans toward themselves, their parents and their background.[9]

The socialization process has been effective in the United States in part because it has had a considerable number of rewards to offer those who complied. We like to believe that our European ancestors left their homelands to escape from religious or political persecution when in fact many more came for economic reasons. The men who populated the United States were a mixed breed of landless sons, losers, success-hungry dreamers, and many others anxious for a second chance.

Economic self-realization became the raison d'être of the republic. For the new Americans to inherit its promise of economic success, they had to learn the language, adopt the life style, and accept the value of work and acquisition.[10] Thus the political socialization process was linked up with the major institutions of American society in establishing a rather successful informal system of rewards and punishments which virtually destroyed most of the cohesive ethnic subcultures within two generations. In that sense, the political socialization of millions of aliens into the American polity is a powerful example of learning and adaptive behavior.

A second reason for the extensive interest in political socialization is that because of the rapid creation of the United States, considerable confusion exists and has existed about the question of citizenship. From a legal standpoint, no nation in history has been as generous in granting full rights of citizenship to outsiders. Yet from the perspective of domestic politics, there is the continuing dilemma as to whether being American is an ideal or just a nationality. People who are deviants from the conventional political or social values are termed "un-American." To call a Frenchman who denied the prevailing orthodoxy un-French would be to invite ridicule on the accuser. A Parliamentary un-British Activities Committee would elicit more humor than a Noel Coward comedy. In the United States, however, this type of political rhetoric exists. It exists because we are, in one sense, still unsure of the effectiveness of our political socialization process and thereby try to create and nourish the anxiety that we must prove ourselves worthy to be citizens in the very land of our birth. The emphasis on civic education is one way that the total society can reaffirm its own commitment to things American.

A third reason for our stress on political socialization is that the United States has one of the few firmly established, quasi-independent, youth cultures in the world. While peer group conformity is powerful nearly everywhere, probably only in America does the youth culture command so much attention, money, and respect.[11] One of the explanations for this culture's success is that American society generally places an inordinate emphasis on youth and the manifestations of youth.

The result is that adult society treats the youth culture as an interest group that must be "co-opted" into the system, or as an heretical sect that must be proselytized into the American faith. The attitudes of young people are continually examined and analyzed by our most sophisticated observers to see how closely they correspond to those of their elders. Only in this way can we forecast the signs of deviation and trouble. However, there is a paradox present in this concern: first, adults seek to perpetuate their value system in their progeny and yet, at the same time, a significant number of adults want to show that they are kindred spirits with the youth culture and its goals. Coming of age in America is a difficult process, especially for the middle-aged and the elderly.

Thus these three major factors—massive immigration, the lack of a secure national identity, and the prevalence of a strong youth culture—have all made the political socialization process a conscious concern of all Americans. In addition, the tensions of creating a new nation and of preserving it during periods of massive technological and social turmoil have placed a heavy burden on the political system. The maintainence of this system is to a large extent as dependent on the effectiveness of its political socialization process as it is on the successful resolution of conflict.

The American as Citizen

For some time, social scientists have attempted to use the term *national character* to explain the psychological coherence of a culture as a whole. In its very vulgar sense, this general approach seems to be closely related to popular ethnic and racial sterotypes that confuse more than they enlighten. Particularly during and immediately after World War II, many authors sought to explain the "aggressiveness" of the Germans or the "submissiveness" of the Russians by examining the child-rearing patterns and other manifestations of national culture. The present state of literature on this subject is in disarray, but nonetheless some important questions were raised. The most basic question remains: are there certain regularities in personality patterns which are manifested in one nation rather than in another? In examining this problem social scientists have used the term *modal personality* to indicate the characteristic forms of behavior that are common or standardized in a given society.[12]

The concept of a modal personality is useful for political socialization because it is a yardstick by which one can measure in a general way what is normal behavior in a particular culture. In some instances, this formulation may be helpful in determining what each society's idea of the good citizen is as well.[13]

One of the most important comparative studies of national culture was done by Gabriel Almond and Sidney Verba. Based on large samplings of adult citizens in the United States, Britain, Italy, Germany, and Mexico, this study identified what may be termed a *modal political personality* in each country. While there is, of course, a tremendous variety of political attitudes and beliefs in the United States, the authors found that the participant political culture prevailed.

The average American citizen tends to follow politics somewhat, is proud of his government, and believes that it has an impact on his life. There is a relatively high level of political efficacy in the United States and citizens feel some sense of satisfaction when they go to the polls to vote. People also expect equal treatment from governmental officials and generally express trust in their judgment. In addition, the American citizen is more willing than his foreign counterparts to enlist the help of others and to form groups to bring about political reform.

Overall, the American citizen as a type has extensive trust in the fairness and benevolence of authority, a high sense of political efficacy, and a willingness to participate in politics to effectuate change. It must be emphasized, however, that there are millions of apathetic and even hostile citizens to whom the political system is unimportant or even malevolent. As will be seen later, children from such subcultures of political cynicism and despair do not share the predominant attitudes so characteristic of children elsewhere in America. However, this sketch of the democratic participant is important for any study of American political socialization because it represents to a large extent the ideal citizen, the goal of much of our intensive education.[14] Table 1.1 summarizes the orientations, activities, and institutions that are characteristic of the participant political culture.

The History of Political Socialization

Because of this increased emphasis on political culture, many scholars have begun to devote more time and attention to the ways in which attitudes are transmitted to the young. However, interest in the political socialization process did not begin with modern social science. It has been a significant concern of philosophers and educators for centuries. Both Plato and Aristotle were quite aware of the importance of the Greek *paideia*, a broad term that encompassed both culture and education. Whether it be Rousseau, Machiavelli, or Dewey, social critics have recognized that the effectiveness of the political system is due in large part to its educational processes. It is no coincidence that the only major philosopher to neglect the socialization process was Hobbes, for whom force and self-interest were sufficient grounds for guaranteeing obedience. Where suasion and inculcation are absent, the state must fall back more quickly on its primary resource—physical coercion.

In the twentieth century in the United States, there have been three major periods of scholarly interest in political socialization.[15] The first was an examination of the formal aspects of civic training done by the American Historical Association in the late 1920s and early 1930s under the editorship of Charles E. Merriam. The Merriam series was an attempt to examine different political systems and to compare their processes of civic education. Special attention was paid to the questions of social cohesion and political loyalty. The Merriam series generally gave central importance to the formal mechanisms of civic education such as the schools, political parties, and governmental agencies, although there was also some investigation of the role of political symbolism and national culture. The second development in the study of political socialization was the attempt to describe and define *national*

Table 1.1
The Participant Political Culture

Orientations	Activities	Institutions
1. Informed 2. Trustful 3. Concern for fellow man 4. Self-esteem 5. Political efficacy 6. Regards authority as benevolent	1. Individual concern about community 2. Joins voluntary associations 3. Active, informed political participation	1. Extensive number of voluntary associations 2. Well-defined interest groups 3. Accessible party system 4. Responsive representation with feedback

character. The third and most recent development is the research that has been done on the political development of children.

In 1959 Herbert Hyman collected and summarized nearly all of the useful studies that dealt with political socialization. Since Hyman's summary, political socialization research projects have proliferated in a variety of locales. The first major study was done by Fred I. Greenstein in the New Haven area and formed the basis for his book, *Children and Politics*. Meanwhile, studies were also being done by Roberta Sigel in Detroit, Joseph Adelson in Ann Arbor, Edgar Litt in Boston, and Kenneth Langton and M. Kent Jennings at the Survey Research Center at the University of Michigan. Most of these studies used the tools of survey research in order to fathom the beliefs and attitudes of children toward politics and the political system.[16]

One of the earliest and most extensive analyses of political socialization was the Chicago Project under the direction of Robert Hess and David Easton.[17] This study was based on a nationwide survey of thousands of predominantly white public school children in grades two to eight. The first volume, written by Hess and Judith Torney, deals with the relationship between political socialization and other variables such as family, school, peer group, class, IQ, religion, and sex. The second volume, written by Easton and Jack Dennis, is formulated within the systems analysis framework. More emphasis is placed on the systemic importance of the political socialization process and how children are inculcated into a shared consensus toward the political community, the regime, and the government.

There are, of course, many other areas of interest that could be investigated by those examining the political socialization process. Generally, however, these areas can be grouped according to their individual or systemic focus. The first set of problem areas would be: political socialization across the life cycle, the political learning process, the extent and relative effects of political socialization upon different individuals, and specialized—especially elite—political socialization. The second set of problem areas would deal more with the political system: the system relevance of the process, political socialization across generations, cross-cultural comparisons, the content taught, subgroup and subcultural variations, and the agents and agencies of political socialization. While this work will touch on all these areas, the primary focus will be on the political socialization process and the life cycle.

These ten areas are not isolated or distinct from one another, but rather they are related in intricate and complex ways. Jack Dennis has tried to show what he terms "the flow influence in political socialization" by using the diagram which is shown in Figure 1.1. While many of the areas that he identifies have not been researched at all, it is still important to realize how broad the political socialization process is and how it affects the larger political system.[18]

Figure 1.1
The Flow of Influence in Political Socialization within a Political System

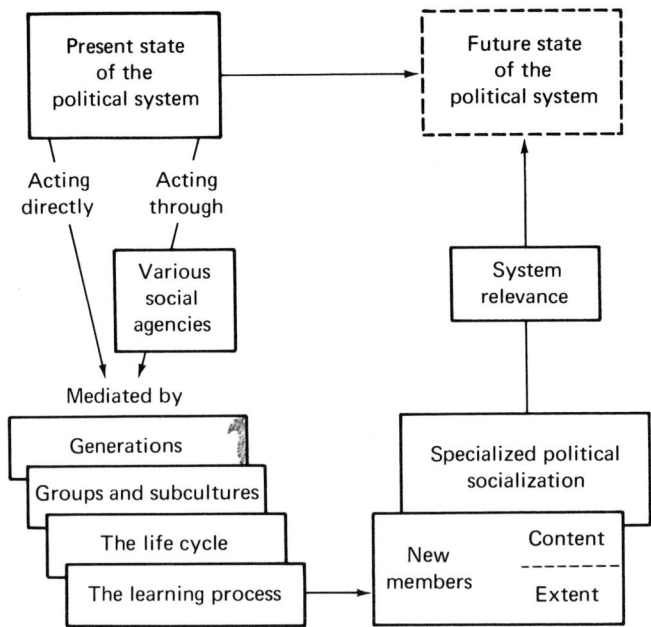

Source: Reprinted from "Major Problems of Political Socialization Research," *Midwest Journal of Political Science*, 12 (February 1968) by Jack Dennis, p. 113, by permission of the Wayne State University Press.

While all of these areas merit consideration, most studies of political socialization have concentrated on three major questions: what are the agents and variables affecting this process, what are the beliefs and attitudes that are inculcated; and how effective is each agent and the total process itself?

The first question seems to be relatively easy to answer: one is affected by family, friends, the media, school, and other formal organizations. While all of these are agents of socialization, the difficulty comes not in enumerating them (although this listing is not comprehensive) but in evaluating their effectiveness. What is most confusing is that it is possible that even if one variable (e.g., family) is isolated and analyzed, its real significance may still go undetected. Many of the findings discussed in the following chapters illustrate this problem.

The second question, which has drawn special attention, is what specific beliefs and attitudes people have toward authority and toward the government. While the modal American citizen has already been described, we must also investigate the subcultures in the United States that do not emphasize the participant style of politics and in which cynicism is more prevalent than trust.

Lastly, there has been some evaluation of how effective the total process itself has been. This is especially important because in times of self-proclaimed crisis and reexamination the political socialization process is usually seen as being a mainstay of stability or at least as an aid in making change as painless as possible.

Before examining these three familiar areas, we must first place the study of political socialization within some sort of conceptual framework. This book seeks to do that by regarding political socialization as only one aspect of the total socialization process—a process that is lifelong and does not cease at the end of adolescence. As Erik Erikson has shown, human beings go through stages of psychological development with each stage having its crises, challenges, and disappointments.[19]

To some extent the same thing is true of political socialization. People develop a sensibility or a mental and emotional responsiveness toward the political community of which they are a part. This sensibility changes as the individual moves through the life cycle. At each stage, there is a reformulation of this sensibility which enables one to conceptualize politics differently. The greatest developments take place during the earliest years of life when psychological and physiological changes occur most rapidly.

It is, of course, difficult to take the life cycle and divide it up into phases or stages of development. In the history of a person such changes are more gradual and less pronounced than any analysis can display. But, for the purpose of this study, we have created a typology which will identify these stages and their characteristics.

One of the biggest problems of political socialization research is that it often seems rigid and frozen. Hopefully, a developmental model will tone down that impression. However, as with any typology, there are other kinds of difficulties that arise. First, we are not suggesting that this typology is universally true regardless of time or place. It is *system specific*, that is, it is based upon research into the political behavior and attitudes of modern Americans.

Second, this typology contains approximate age levels. Obviously, the development of people varies considerably and these ages are only, at best, modal levels for each stage. Actually, the main reason why these age levels are included is to enable us to approximate, even in a rough way, when most changes seem to occur.

Third, it must be acknowledged that stage theories of any kind do have a certain rigidity of their own.[20] Oftentimes one gets the impression that all of mankind is moving in lockstep throughout life. In addition, there are also some problems as to how physiological changes relate to psychological changes and how both of them influence political behavior.

For our purposes, we may narrow down these problems to two basic questions: first, must a certain stage of political socialization be preceded by certain physiological developments, and second, do certain physiological developments necessarily bring forth certain stages in political development?

As for the first question, it is obvious that during the latent or early stages of political socialization the child's ability to conceptualize and identify is heavily dependent upon certain physiological changes. A child who has only developed to the growth stage of age five or so is not going to be able to comprehend the complexities of politics. But as we move away from the apparent examples, it appears that in the more manifest stages the physiological aspects become less crucial. For example, a student who "should be" at the stage of passive participation may actually be involved in many ways in the intricacies of politics.

Yet these exceptions can easily be overemphasized. As a person develops there are certain crisis points in life, and these points involve a mixture of physiological aging, psychic adjustment, and social role. Puberty, the search for identity, marriage, parenthood, vocational adjustment, and old age are all distinct periods in life. Thus, while the linkage between the stages of political socialization and physiological change are not ironclad, especially after adolescence, there is still a strong and reciprocal relationship between them.

The second question deals with the other dimension of development: must certain physiological changes bring forth a specific political stage? On the basis of what has been said above, the answer must be negative. The first sort of changes merely create a state of readiness during which the latter can occur with some ease and greater predictability.

It should not be forgotten that the political world is a set of conventions which help structure the environment. For example, as we will see later, retired people tend to disengage themselves from politics. But it is quite possible to create a political system where the leadership positions would be monopolized by the oldest, able-bodied people and in which advancing age would be associated with wisdom rather than with senility. In such a situation this disengagement phenomenon would not be a part of the political sensibility.

This sequence of stages of development is useful in enabling us to see the variations and characteristics of such changes. However, there is one last caveat that must be made. When a person reaches a particular stage of development, he may react in either a prosystemic or an antisystemic way. The development of a political sensibility at any stage in the life cycle does not imply loyalty to the system. One can be either cynical or trusting, participant or apathetic, or somewhere in between.

The positive and negative manifestations of this sensibility can be equally justifiable responses. Political socialization studies, like most of political science, have a heavy establishment bias. While it is probably not possible to dispel that prosystemic emphasis, it is still best to remember that negative responses are possible and may even be, under certain circumstances, more morally correct.

The Typology

Table 1.2 summarizes the typology along the lines we have indicated. It divides the stages of development into two categories—latent and manifest. The first three stages are latent ones in which the young child acquires early predispositions that have a direct bearing on how he continues to perceive human relationships and social regulation. The last seven stages include the more manifest aspects of development when a person comes to relate to the community, the nation, and its formal institutions. There is, of course, some overlap between the latent and manifest categories and we will deal with this in the next chapter. These ten stages may be summarized as follows.

Stage I—Imitation

One of the most important ways that a child first learns is by imitating models, usually the adults around him. In his early relationships with those models, the child develops feelings of trust (or mistrust) which remain a part of his personality.

Stage II—Command Morality

The rules which adults lay down to govern a child's behavior become his first experience with formal social regulations. At this age the child believes that such rules and regulations are unalterable and eternal commands that can only be disobeyed with the gravest consequences. In this way, an element of certainty becomes part of his social life.

Stage III—Consensus Morality

As the child matures he begins to enlarge his circle of acquaintances to include playmates as well as family. The child also begins to see that rules should represent the common decisions of all involved and that laws should be fair.

Table 1.2
Stages in the Development of the Political Sensibility

Stage	Age	Focal point	Positive manifestation	Negative manifestation
Latent				
I. Imitation	0-6	Mother/caretaker	Trust	Mistrust
II. Command Morality	6-9	Ideal elder	Absolute laws	Uncertainty
III. Consensus Morality	7-10+	Peer group	Common decisions	Power assertive
Manifest				
IV. Communitarianism	7-10+	Community	Common good	Egoism
V. Abstract Allegiance	10-12	Nation-state	Unity, national primacy	Apathy
VI. Civic Awareness	12-16	Government	Beneficial functions	Cynicism
VII. Passive and Active Participation	16-18	Political process	General operational awareness	Sense of inefficacy
VIII. Preparatory Leadership	18-30	Political issues and controversies	Patriotic identification	Lack of identification
IX. Generational Leadership	30-60	Problems of governance	National destiny	Nonparticipation
X. Retrospective Leadership	60—	The nation in history	Transcendence and continuity	Isolation and despair

Stage IV—Communitarianism

While the child's attitudes toward law and responsibility are changing, so too are his views about social relations. By the time he enters school, the young citizen is developing a manifest political sensibility. He sees himself as being a part of a larger community and he stresses its harmony and general objectives. Usually he is willing to subordinate his own egoism and self-interest to what he is taught is the common good.

Stage V—Abstract Allegiance

The child's notion of the political community changes from a general kind of amorphous identification to a specific sort of national allegiance. He comes to realize the uniqueness of his political system vis-à-vis the others in the world. Depending on his orientation, the child develops either a strong concern or a general apathy toward his nation's unity and preeminence.

Stage VI—Civic Awareness

By the beginning of his early teens the individual becomes more aware of the specific activities of the government and whether it affects people in benevolent or malevolent ways.

Stage VII—Passive and Active Participation

As he matures the adolescent begins to see how the political process actually operates and what the role of the citizen is. The majority of adolescents take a rather passive view toward political participation and concentrate instead on problems of social adjustment during this time. But there is a minority that begins to become aware and active in either supportive or disruptive ways.

Stage VIII—Preparatory Leadership

When the young citizen is finally allowed to participate fully he is usually slow in getting involved. While there is some concern with political controversies, most people at this age level are still more concerned with courtship and vocational preparation than with the public's business except when it directly affects their lives.

Stage IX—Generational Leadership

Once established, a person becomes more concerned with politics and is more likely to participate in its workings as either a leader or a follower than he was previously. It is also at this stage that some individuals begin to think of what destiny or mission their nation is supposed to have. Some seek out a larger or smaller frame of reference (such as world federalism or ethnic solidarity), but still it is this age group that provides the preponderance of people with such a concern—although some of these sentiments are manifested in the previous two stages in lesser proportions.

Stage X—Retrospective Leadership

Old age leads to a gradual retrenchment of the elderly from the life of the community, including politics. The elderly then develop either a strong concern about the transcendence of the community over death, or they lose themselves in a world of loneliness, isolation, and despair.

Summary

This chapter has explored the reasons why Americans have been so concerned with political socialization and civic education. The more recent studies have provided us with a considerable amount of evidence on the effects that various agents and influences have on the socialization process.

The remaining chapters seek to place this information in a developmental framework. Such a framework identifies the particular characteristics of each stage and shows how socialization is a continuing process that ceases only at death.

Notes

1. A good example of the wolf children literature is Reverend J. A. L. Singh and Professor Robert M. Zingg, *Wolf-Children and Feral Man* (Hamden, Conn.: Archon Press, 1966). Aristotle's observation is in his *Politics* (New York: Modern Library, 1943), book I, chapter 3, p. 55.

2. Edward Zigler and Irvin L. Child, "Socialization," *The Handbook of Social Psychology*, edited by Gardner Lindzey and Elliot Aronson, 2d ed. (Reading: Addison-Wesley, 1969), pp. 450-589.

3. The most familiar formulation of this view is Sigmund Freud, *Civilization and Its Discontents* (New York: Norton, 1961). A related plea for extending the political imagination is Henry Kariel, *Open Systems* (Ithaca, Illinois: Peacock Publishers, 1969).

4. To a certain extent, the United States has already reached this point of artificial scarcity. See: J. K. Galbraith, *The New Industrial State* (Boston: Houghton Mifflin, 1967);Herbert Marcuse, *Eros and Civilization* (New York: Vintage, 1962); and Herbert Marcuse, *One-Dimensional Man*(Boston: Beacon Press, 1968).

5. A more comprehensive study of the conservative view toward society and convention is presented in Robert Nisbet, *The Sociological Tradition* (New York: Basic Books, 1966).

6. Roberta S. Sigel, "Image of the Presidency—Part II of an Exploration Into Popular Views of Presidential Power," *Midwest Journal of Political Science*, 10 (February 1966), 123-37 and Fred I. Greenstein, "The Benevolent Leader: Children's Image

of Political Authority," *American Political Science Review* 54 (December 1960), 934-943.

7. Milton H. Fried, *The Evolution of Political Society* (New York: Random House, 1967), pp. 5-7.

8. For a discussion of the concept of politics, see David Easton, *The Political System* (New York: Knopf, 1953), pp. 129-131. Different explorations are Murray Edelman, *Symbolic Uses of Politics* (Urbana: University of Illinois Press, 1967) and Ernst Cassirer, *The Philosophy of Symbolic Forms* (New Haven: Yale University Press, 1953), 3 volumes.

9. The most popular study of immigrants in America is Nathan Glazer and Daniel Moynihan, *Beyond the Melting Pot* (Cambridge, Mass.: MIT Press, 1966). A good study of persistent ethnic ties is Edgar Litt, *Beyond Pluralism* (Glenview, Ill.: Scott, Foresman, 1970).

10. Robert Lane's *Political Ideology* (New York: Free Press, 1962) is a superb in-depth account of the attitudes of fifteen citizens on various questions, including equality.

11. Elton B. McNeil, *Human Socialization* (Belmont: Brooks/Cole, 1969). The importance of the youth culture is stressed by Theodore Roszak, *The Making of a Counter Culture* (New York: Anchor, 1969) and Charles Reich, *The Greening of America* (New York: Randon House, 1970).

12. A summary of national character literature is found in Alex Inkeles and Daniel J. Levinson, "National Character: The Study of Modal Personality and Sociocultural Systems," *The Handbook of Social Psychology*, Lindzey and Aronson, pp. 418-506.

13. While the modal personality concept may sometimes indicate what the ideal citizenship model is, it must be remembered that the first concept is a statistical one and the latter is a philosophical one. It is likely that in certain subcultures the modal personality may be quite different from the formal ideal of a good citizen.

14. Gabriel Almond and Sidney Verba, *The Civic Culture* (Princeton, N.J.: Princeton University Press, 1963). Figure 1.1 is based upon the characteristics of a participant culture described in this work. Of course, it is possible for a society less complex than the United States to be participant and yet lack many of these characteristics, especially *formalized* institutions of interest articulation.

15. Fred I. Greenstein, "Political Socialization," *International Encyclopedia of the Social Sciences* (New York: Crowell Collier, 1969), p. 552. Three of the most relevant volumes in the Merriam Series are Charles Merriam, *The Making of Citizens* (Chicago: University of Chicago Press, 1931); Charles Merriam, *Civic Education in the United States* (New York: Scribner, 1934); and Bessie Louise Pierce, *Civic Attitudes in American School Textbooks* (Chicago: University of Chicago Press, 1930.)

16. A useful summary is provided in Judith V. Torney, "Chronology of Data Collection and Publications in Political Socialization," *The Learning of Political Behavior*, edited by Norman Adler and Charles Harrington (Glenview,Ill.: Scott, Foresman, 1970), pp. 193-196.

17. Robert D. Hess and David Easton, "The Child's Changing Image of the President," *Public Opinion Quarterly*, 24 (Winter 1960), 632–644; Hess and Judith V. Torney, *The Development of Political Attitudes* (New York: Anchor, 1967); David Easton and Robert D. Hess, "The Child's Political World," *Midwest Journal of Political Science*, 6 (August 1962), 229–46; and Easton and Dennis, *Children in the Political System* (New York: McGraw-Hill, 1969).

18. Jack Dennis, "Major Problems of Political Socialization Research," *Midwest*

Journal of Political Science, 12 (February 1968), 85–114. For those who are more interested in the systemic aspects of political socialization, Richard Dawson and Kenneth Prewitt, *Political Socialization* (Boston: Little Brown, 1969) and Richard Merelman, *Political Socialization and Educational Climates* (New York: Holt, 1971) are most useful in this regard.

19. Erik Erikson's work is of major interest to anyone concerned with stage theories of personality. His two best known works are *Youth: Identity and Crisis* (New York: Norton, 1968) and *Childhood and Society* (New York: Norton, 1950).

20. One good critique of stage theories is William Kessen, " 'Stage' and 'Structure' in the Study of Children," *Cognitive Development in Children* (Chicago: University of Chicago Press, 1970), pp. 55–72.

21. A succinct and interesting discussion of this problem of bias can be found in Fred I. Greenstein, "A Note on the Ambiguity of 'Political Socialization': Definitions, Criticism, and Strategies of Inquiry," *Journal of Politics,* 32 (November 1970), 969–978.

two

The Stirrings of Moral Authority

At first, it may seem unnecessary to discuss the child in his earliest and admittedly prepolitical phases of development. Yet it is during these periods that a child develops his first conceptual framework and his first feelings of self-esteem, trust, efficacy, guilt, and fairness.

Parents, looking at their helpless infant, often assume that he is a passive and confused recipient of an endless stream of novel stimuli.[1] However, in the last twenty or thirty years psychologists have discovered increasing evidence that the child, even in his first months of life, is far more aware than had previously been realized. In fact, even his visual skills are more developed than adult observers had commonly assumed.

One of the most perceptive investigators of child behavior for the last several decades has been Jean Piaget. Piaget has found that the newborn infant often initiates activity himself and is already modifying his behavior on the basis of one month's life experience. It seems that the infant is seeking to structure his psychological environment so that he may deal with it in an organized or coherent way. In examining the early behavior patterns of an infant, one can see how learning quickly leads to modifications even in such reflex activities as sucking, swallowing and crying.[2]

Piaget first examined these modifications (called *assimilation*) by observing the sucking reflexes of his son, Laurent. Piaget found that any organism has a basic tendency to exercise its organizing structure: that is, to make it function. In the case of Laurent, Piaget observed that his son sucked not just because he was hungry, but because he had developed a tendency to make use of behavior patterns once they were established. Piaget realized that Laurent later came to generalize this behavior to other objects, such as blankets, toys, and fingers. Then, as he developed, the infant began to exercise selectivity or discrimination in choosing objects to suck on.[3]

The importance of Piaget's observations is that they indicate that even the one-month-old infant can learn from experience and adapt his behavior in rather sophisticated ways. This ability of a person to assimilate and change his behavior patterns is crucial to survival.

Imitation

Another way that children and adults attempt to comprehend reality and deal with their environment is by imitation. The more one examines the imitation process, the more one realizes its complexity. Yet even at the earliest age, the infant can be seen imitating other people's behavior. At first, he can only imitate a person who is directly in front of him. But later, after the first year, it seems that the infant can remember and imitate the behavior of people he had seen previously.

In the imitation process, there are many different types of people who may serve as models: superiors in an age group hierarchy, superiors in a hierarchy of social status, superiors in an intelligence ranking system, and superior technicians in any field.[4] In the case of the infant, he is most likely to imitate those nearset to him during his early years. The process of imitation is important in explaining adult behavior as well. In fact, any discussion of the relationship between leaders and followers must take into account two different types of imitation. The first is called *matched-dependent behavior* and occurs when the leader is able to read the relevant environmental cues, but his followers are not. The second type of imitation is *copying* and involves a learner who is trying to reproduce the behavior of his model.[5] Any one desiring to understand the dynamics of leadership must be aware of both of these types of imitative behavior.[6]

For the purposes of this study, imitation is examined because it represents the first stage in the development of the political sensibility. But even though imitation is crucial in explaining childhood behavior, we never totally leave behind our desire or our need to emulate others.* For example, Arnold

---

*Various scholars have noted that historical figures tend to imitate more ancient heroes. For example, one of Napoleon's models was Julius Caesar; Caesar's was Alexander; and Alexander's was the Homeric hero Achilles. Thus one can see the peculiar links between the so-called mythical and the real worlds. It very well may be that the impetus for the emergence of the hero in history lies not so much in the dynamics of events, but rather in the unconscious imitation of our own mythical projections.

Toynbee, in his study of civilizations, has found that imitation or *mimesis* is one of the most important historical processes. Toynbee maintains that mimesis is the tool or "social drill" which the creative minority uses to move the majority in particular directions. It is one way of achieving genuine social cohesiveness which avoids the intricacies and delays of political dialogue and endless consultation. However, when these minorities lose their creative abilities and become decadent this process leads to mechanization and finally disintegration.[7]

The importance of imitative behavior can be seen rather clearly in our own society. Through the political socialization process defenders of the social order seek to inculcate in the young patterns of behavior which correspond to certain models of orthodox patriotism. It is for this reason that educators place such an emphasis on heroes and their feats in teaching history. What were once minor events in a man's life or in the life of his generation become glorified and fabled for the sake of posterity.

The child is told to emulate or imitate the behavior and the attitudes of appropriate leaders. However, what often happens is that there are many models that can be emulated. Children come to know and imitate not just patriots, but villains as well. They not only become acquainted with the deeds of great men but also with the activities of the lesser men who populate their neighborhoods.

During certain periods of life, especially in early adolescence, it seems that the fashions of peer groups rather than the demands of citizenship command most of the young's imitative inclinations. Nevertheless, imitation is an indispensable tool of socializaton, vital not just in the inculcation of children but also for the very cohesiveness of society in general.

Trust and Efficacy

The process of imitation and the general propensity of people (and animals) to learn have been found to be facilitated by the use of reward and praise as methods of reinforcement. Even in our own adult lives, we are more likely to respond affirmatively to those who relate to us in positive ways.[8] So too, the young child responds more quickly and more lastingly to such methods of reinforcement in his desire to make and keep his world as benevolent and dependable as possible.

The importance of regularity and dependability for the helpless infant is obvious. In his earliest months he develops an underlying sense of either trust or mistrust based on his daily experiences, usually with his mother. Examining this period, Erik Erikson has observed that in "adults a radical impairment of basic trust and a prevalence of basic mistrust is expressed in a particular form of severe estrangement which characterizes individuals who withdraw into themselves when at odds with themselves and with others."[9]

As will be seen later, a sense of trust (or mistrust) is important in understanding a child's basic orientation toward authority and the political system in general. From the research that has been done on this topic, it seems that political trust (or mistrust) is a function of a broader feeling about the benevolence of one's environment. In addition, feelings of trust are closely related to a sense of personal efficacy and self-esteem. Efficacy is the feeling that one's efforts can produce a desirable effect; such a feeling is an obvious reflection of how much confidence and social worth a person thinks he possesses. These levels of trust, esteem, and efficacy are important antecedents of social behavior and political participation.

An obvious example is that the more efficacious a person feels, the more he will try to accomplish and the more he will eventually succeed in doing. A positive orientation is not only an antecedent of success but one of its main causes. Whether one likes it or not, it is as logical as it is unjust that the child who has had a rewarding past will be likely to have a fruitful future.

The importance of the efficacy-esteem-trust triad to political participation is well documented. Those citizens with feelings of efficacy and esteem are more likely to participate in the political process.* In addition, some sociologists have maintained that those with a high sense of trust and efficacy are less likely to be authoritarian and more likely to be tolerant of political and social differences. Such politically relevant attitudes obviously are grounded in the broader life experiences which a person undergoes.[10]

Concepts of Rules

Because he prizes a dependable and regular environment, the young child comes to place primary emphasis on rules. The major investigator of rule behavior in children is again Piaget, who has studied the ways in which the game of marbles is played. The first type of rules which the child observes when he tries to assimilate the marble into his earlier schema is motor rules. However, Piaget's real motive in investigating the rituals of play is to discern the central characteristics of rule behavior.

If a child's behavior is to have some moral (and social) significance, then

*An interesting critique of this line of thought is Harold Lasswell's hypothesis that power seekers are likely to be those who are trying to compensate for their personal failures and feelings of low esteem by projecting their needs onto the public arena. See his *Power and Personality* (New York: Viking, 1948), chap. 3.

obviously rules must be linked to some network of obligations between people. To examine this aspect, Piaget began to observe and question children about their activities. He found that between the ages of two and five the child begins to receive, from the outside world, examples of codified rules, as in the case of the game of marbles. Piaget described the process in the following way.

> But though the child imitates this example, he continues to play either by himself without bothering to find play-fellows, or with others, but without trying to win, and therefore without attempting to unify the different ways of playing. In other words, children of this stage, even when they are playing together, play each one "on his own" (everyone can win at once) and without regard for any codification of rules. This dual character, combining imitation of others with a purely individual use of the examples received, we have designated by the term Egocentrism.[11]

This sort of activity is really midway between purely individual and formal social behavior. The young child, in the Imitation stage, desires to play like the other children he sees, especially those older than himself. Yet the child is really still playing by himself, thinking that his unique style is right and correct.* Observing this, Piaget commented that the "true socius" of the player at this stage of development is not his flesh and blood partner, but the ideal and abstract elder whom the child inwardly strives to imitate and who sums up all the examples he has ever received.[12]

As the child matures somewhat, he leaves this stage and enters a second one, that of Command Morality. It is at this point that children come to harbor an almost "mystical respect for rules: rules are eternal, due to the authority of the parents, of the Gentlemen of the Commune, and even of Almighty God. It is forbidden to change them, and even if the whole of general opinion supported a change, general opinion would be in the wrong: the unanimous consent of all children would be powerless against the truth of Tradition."[13]

It is also during this period of Command Morality that the child develops a unilateral respect for authority and a real awareness of the prestige of his superiors. However, the child still does not establish a genuine mutual contact with the adult; he remains shut up within his own ego. What occurs

---

*Piaget also points up the interesting types of conversations that occur between children (from two to six), which he calls "collective monologues." These children, while desiring the presence of others, seem to speak only to themselves. What the adult sees then is the interesting spectacle of two children talking aloud at the same time in the other's presence, yet each perfectly content with the non-dialogue.

is that while the child submits more or less completely in intention to the prescribed rules, these rules remain external to his conscience. They do not really transform his conduct. This explains why the rules seem sacred but often are not put into practice.

There is some variation among children, but it appears that after a year or two at this phase of Command Morality, attitudes again begin to alter and become somewhat more sophisticated. The child develops a desire for some sort of mutual understanding in the sphere of play. While before the child sought first to imitate others and then to respect those rules that were handed down to him, he now begins to place more emphasis on cooperating with his peers.

It is this development which marks the beginning of Stage III—Consensus Morality. Children begin to cooperate with each other even though they are competing against one another. While they do not yet know the rules in detail (at ages seven to ten), they try as best they can to adhere to their mutually agreed upon framework. As they grow older, these children begin to cooperate in even more obvious ways and their attitudes toward rules change considerably. The rules of the game are no longer sacred laws laid down by outside adults. Instead, they are the outcome of free decisions made by the children themselves. Changes in the rules are allowed as long as the other participants agree. Piaget remarks that "democracy follows on theocracy and gerontocracy: there are no crimes of opinion, but only breaches in procedure. All opinions are tolerated so long as their protagonists urge their acceptance by legal methods."[14]

By the age of ten or eleven, children come to place an increased emphasis upon codification and complete application of the law. The child begins, in a rudimentary way, to realize the basic functions of law and its relationship to reciprocity and fairness. Considerable emphasis is placed on the point that no one has the right to introduce innovation except by the legal methods of persuasion and majority rule. It is at this age that a child begins more fully to acquire ideas about the political community of which they are a part.[15]

Making Moral Judgments

Not only do the attitudes that children have toward rules change, but even their understanding of morality alters as they grow older. During the stage of Command Morality, children believe that rules cannot be questioned or doubted; they are more concerned with the exact letter of the law than with its spirit or intention. For them, goodness is defined as strict obedience to the rules, which in turn create categorical obligations that are always applicable.

The child under ten has an objective concept of responsibility. He usually does not assess the importance of motive but judges actions by how well they conform to the established rules. To demonstrate that point, Piaget told some children several stories and asked them to make moral judgments about each story. In one story, a young boy accidentally knocked over a tray with fifteen cups on it and broke all of them. In the second story, a boy broke one cup when he tried to get some jam out of the cupboard before his mother found out. The respondents under age ten usually chose the first boy as being the most culpable—because he had broken more cups. The question of motive begins to emerge only in the thinking of children above the age of nine. To the child of six or seven, the objective concept of responsibility seems to be more justified.[16]

As the child matures and his concepts about rules change, so too does his moral jugdment. In the Consensus stage, the child becomes more able to assess the importance of motive in human conduct.[17] As he grows older, especially after the age of ten, the child begins to realize that truthfulness is necessary not only to avoid punishment, but also because deception destroys mutual trust and the possibility of cooperation. Thus he moves away from the absolute morality of right and duty toward a morality of goodness in which cooperation and moral autonomy are possible.[18]

Lastly, the child's concept of justice also undergoes reexamination. Basically, children maintain that four kinds of actions are unfair or unjust: behavior that is forbidden by adults; behavior that goes against the rules of the game; behavior that violates equality; and acts of adult injustice (economic and political). When these four kinds of actions are broken down into categories, there are some very interesting variations by age; younger children place a greater emphasis on adult approval while older children stress equality and social justice. (See Table 2.1.)

Table 2.1
Types of Injustice

Age	Forbidden	Games	Inequality	Social injustice
6-8	64%	9%	27%	—
9-12	7	9	73	11%

Source: Jean Piaget, *The Moral Judgment of the Child* (New York: Free Press, 1965), p. 314. Copyright © 1965 by the Macmillan Company.

Up to the age of seven or eight the child equates justice with the commands of adult authority. He makes no distinctions between justice, duty, and obedience; every punishment is therefore legitimate and morally correct. In his mind authority takes precedence over any other consideration. But after seven or eight there is a progressive development of the child's physical and psychological autonomy. He begins to feel that the principle of equality is an important aspect of social relationships. Along with this, his views on punishment also change; more emphasis is placed on reciprocal obligation than on personal retribution. In addition, at this age the child is more willing to look at the circumstances surrounding an act before determining whether or not it is just.[19]

While it is important to point out the changes that occur in childhood conceptualization, it must be remembered that notions such as reciprocity, obligation, justice, and duty are rather complex and that the young child is dealing with them in only the most rudimentary of ways. While there is still a considerable amount of moral development that takes place in the later years, we have examined these first three stages more closely because they are important first steps in the development of a political sensibility. By the time the child passes the age of seven or eight, he begins to acquire attitudes about politics and authority which are more manifest and which will be discussed later. Yet even in adulthood this continuing moral development does have a tangential effect on political and social behavior.

It is really not possible to follow both the moral and political development of a person without a great deal of confusion. So let us give a very brief overview of postchildhood moral change by concluding with the findings of Lawrence Kohlberg and his associates. Using Piaget's basic approach, Kohlberg in one study examined seventy-two boys from the ages of ten to sixteen to determine their moral development.[20] He found that at first the child responds to cultural rules and categories of right and wrong in terms of whether an action will bring punishment or reward. The child gradually moves away from this view and becomes more concerned with fairness and sharing because he sees that he can receive reciprocal benefits under this arrangement. Later on the child begins to become more aware of the expectations of his family, his group, and his community or nation. He desires to conform to their image of what a good child is supposed to be like. In addition, the child begins to stress his loyalty to the major authority figures in society and to the maintenance of the social order.

As the individual begins to enter the early years of adulthood, moral values and principles become more important to him. He begins to understand the relative nature of personal opinions and value judgments. At the same time, more of an emphasis is placed on procedure and the belief that changes should only be made through specific channels and on the basis of social utility.

In some cases, the individual may even progress further to the highest plateau of moral development, which Kohlberg calls "the universal ethical orientation." The principles which are a part of this orientation are justice, equality, and a respect for individual dignity.

Kohlberg does not argue that eventually everyone reaches the highest plateau; in fact, probably only a tenth of the adult population will ever adopt the universal ethical orientation. In addition, many people regress or are fixated at particular levels. But he does argue, rather convincingly, that the *sequence* of moral development is invariable. Based on his studies in the United States, Taiwan, Mexico, and Turkey, Kohlberg has found that while there is some variation in the time of development in each country (and in different classes), nonetheless the sequence remains the same.[21]

Studies like those done by Piaget and Kohlberg are quite relevant to any analysis of political socialization. These findings give us important data on how children think and on how notions of morality, law and reciprocity develop. Yet it is important to realize that each person undergoes such a tremendous variety of experiences that it cannot be said that the adult is merely the child writ large.[22]

Summary

This chapter has examined the development of the political sensibility through the early periods of a child's maturation. These first three stages are prepolitical, but they are important in explaining how a person comes to acquire early in life basic attitudes and beliefs about social concepts and relationships. These developments may be summarized as shown in Table 2.2.

This chapter has examined only in very broad strokes the latent stages of development. But even at these stages, the child is living in a social world in which the influences of the family and the total environment begin to cut across neat generalizations about causality and behavior. The patterns of development become more complex as one progresses and the processes of manifest political socialization begin to become more apparent and important.

Table 2.2
Latent Political Phases and the Development of Social Concepts

Stage	Age	Focus	Rules	Justice	Responsibility	Punishment	Morality	Obligation
I. Imitation	0-6	Model	Motor	—	—	Disapproval	Trust	Rudimentary utilitarianism
II. Command	6-9	Ideal elder	Eternal, absolute	Obedience	Objective	Retributive	Duty	Categorical
III. Consensus	7-10+	Peer group	Common decisions	Fairness	Subjective	Reciprocity	Good	Circumstantial

Development of the concept of:

Notes

1. There is increasing evidence that infants can be conditioned at birth or soon after. One study has attempted to show how infants are conditioned even in the womb. See Burton L. White, *Human Infants* (Englewood Cliffs, N.J.: Prentice-Hall, 1971).

2. A fine summary of Piaget's work is Herbert Ginsburg and Sylvia Opper, *Piaget's Theory of Intellectual Development* (Englewood Cliffs, N.J.: Prentice-Hall, 1969). Of major importance is Michael A. Wallach, "Research on Children's Thinking," *Child Psychology*, edited by Harold W. Stevenson (Chicago: University of Chicago Press, 1963), pp. 236–276.

3. Jean Piaget, *The Origins of Intelligence in Children* (New York: International Universities Press, 1952), pp. 23–42.

4. N. E. Miller and J. Dollard, *Social Learning and Imitation* (New Haven: Yale Univeristy Press, 1941), p. 183.

5. Miller and Dollard, p. 11. The importance of imitation is examined also in Albert Bandura and Richard H. Walters, *Social Learning and Personality Development* (New York: Holt, 1963).

6. In many cases such imitation may be incidental to the main activities of the model. See Albert Bandura and Aletha C. Huston, "Identification as a Process of Incidental Learning" *Journal of Abnormal and Social Psychology*, 63 (1961), 311–318.

7. Arnold J. Toynbee, *A Study of History*, vol. I (New York: Dell, 1969), p. 68 passim.

8. Justin Aronfreed, *Conduct and Conscience* (New York: Academic, 1968), pp. 128–129.

9. Erik Erikson develops his concept of trust in his *Identity: Youth and Crisis* (New York: Norton, 1968). pp. 96–106 and in *Childhood and Society* (New York: Norton, 1950), pp. 219–222.

10. Gabriel Almond and Sidney Verba, *The Civic Culture* (Princeton: Princeton University Press, 1963), p. 285; Morris Rosenberg, "Self Esteem and Concern with Public Affairs," *Public Opinion Quarterly*, 26 (Summer 1962), 201–211. On authoritarianism see the conflicting conclusions of Robert Lane, "Political Personality and Electoral Choice," *American Political Science Review*, 49 (March 1955), 173–190 and Morris Janowitz and Dwaine Marvick, "Authoritarianism and Political Behavior," *Public Opinion Quarterly*, 17 (Summer 1953), 185–201. Also of interest are Robert E. Agger, Marshall Goldstein, and Stanley Pearl, "Political Cynicism: Measurement and Meaning," *Journal of Politics*, 23 (August 1961), 477–506 and Edgar Litt, "Political Cynicism and Political Futility," *Journal of Politics*, 25 (May 1963), 312–323.

11. Jean Piaget, *The Moral Judgment of the Child* (New York: Free Press, 1965), p. 27.

12. Piaget, *Moral Judgment*, p. 41.
13. Piaget, *Moral Judgment*, p. 61.
14. Piaget, *Moral Judgment*, p. 65.
15. Piaget, *Moral Judgment*, p. 71.
16. Piaget, *Moral Judgment*, p. 111. Also see the studies of L. Boehn and M. L. Nass, "Social Class Differences in Conscience Development," *Child Development*, 33 (1962), 565–575 and R. MacRae, "A Test of Piaget's Theories of Moral Development," *Journal of Abnormal and Social Psychology*, 49 (1954), 14–18.
17. Piaget, *Moral Judgment*, p. 138.
18. Piaget, *Moral Judgment*, p. 195, and D. Durkin, "Children's Concept of

Justice: A Comparison with the Piaget Data," *Child Development*, 30 (1959), 59–67. R. Johnson, "A Study of Children's Moral Judgments," *Child Development*, 33 (1962), 327–354.

19. Piaget, *Moral Judgment*, pp. 251–262. Also G. R. Medinnus, "Immanent Justice in Children: A Review of the Literature and Additional Data," *Journal of Genetic Psychology*, 90 (1959), 253–262.

20. Kohlberg's work is presented in several sources. See his "Moral Development and Identification," *Child Psychology*, edited by Harold W. Stevenson, pp. 277–332. Also his fine review of the literature on moral character, "Development of Moral Character and Moral Ideology," *Review of Child Development Research*, vol. 1 edited by M. L. Hoffman and Lois W. Hoffman (New York: Russell Sage Foundation, 1964), pp. 383–431. An interesting comparative study is discussed in Kohlberg and R. Kramer, "Continuities and Discontinuities in Childhood and Adult Moral Development," *Human Development*, 12 (1969), 93–120.

21. Kohlberg and Kramer, "Continuities and Discontinuities in Childhood" 100–105. The child's moral development along these lines may not be due, as the authors believe, to his cognitive development. Perhaps, in all societies, adults change their moral vocabulary to fit the age group to which they are talking. Thus the changes in moral sentiment which seem to take place are not so much due to the child as to the adult whom he imitates. This hypothesis is being examined by Dr. Nancy Denny at the University of Kansas.

22. Although this study does not deal with the biological aspects of development in any detail, it is obvious that there is a relationship between biology and political behavior. The exact dimensions of this problem are rather complex and are being explored by various social scientists. The best summary article on the subject is Peter A. Corning, "The Biological Bases of Behavior and Some Implications for Political Science," *World Politics*, 23 (April 1971), 321–370. Also of interest are T. L. Thorson, *Biopolitics* (New York: Holt, 1970); James C. Davies, *Human Nature in Politics* (New York: Wiley, 1963); Albert Somit, "Toward a More Biologically Oriented Political Science: Ethology and Psychopharmacology," *Midwest Journal of Political Science*, 12 (November 1968), 550–567; and Ralph P. Hummel, "Teaching Political Theory: The Impact of Biopolitics," (Unpublished paper, delivered at the American Political Science Association Meeting, September 7–11, 1971). Other more popularized works of interest are: Konrad Lorenz, *On Aggression* (New York: Bantam, 1970); Robert Ardrey, *The Territorial Imperative* (New York: Dell, 1968); and Lionel Tiger and Robin Fox, *Imperial Animal* (New York: Holt, 1971).

three

The Family as Predisposition

During the early years in the life of a child, four mechanisms aid in his socialization: a propensity for imitation; the ability to identify with those he respects and loves; a strong desire for affection and regard; and a fear of punishment. These mechanisms make the child greatly dependent on the approval of the adults who oversee his life. He adjusts his activities to conform to their wishes and, in the process, begins to develop a sort of rudimentary utilitarian view of life; that is, that one should seek pleasure and avoid pain.[1]

In his dealings with the adult world, the child seeks models and imitates their behavior and often their very mannerisms. His first models of identification are those people nearest to him. In our society these people are the members of the nuclear family.[2] In Chapter 2 we saw how this propensity to imitate is really the first stage in the development of a political sensibility because it enables the child to come to grips with some of the social realities that influence his life. Furthermore, this tendency to imitate is not merely a phase that one outgrows but a habit which remains a part of adult behavior patterns as well.

Albert Bandura and his associates have found that when children are exposed to models who display aggressive behavior, the children too seem to display aggression—especially if it seems that the model's behavior is rewarded. However, while the young child can imitate the behavior of many different adults, generally he chooses as his model the most nurturant person in his life. In our society this person is usually the child's mother because it is she who is most concerned with his problems and needs.[3]

The Problems of Predisposition

There was a time when psychologists used a genetic argument when trying to explain the antecedents of adult behavior. Since the family is the central social institution during these early, formative years, it seemed logical that adult personalities were directly molded by childhood experiences. But because of the complexities of adult development, students of personality have generally become more cautious in making such neat causal statements.

While there is no comprehensive theory of personality, some important generalizations can be made about the basic predispositions which the family is able to inculcate in the child. Attitudes like aggressiveness, tolerance, trust, and self-esteem are transmitted to the child and help to form his early personality.

One of the problems in evaluating the effects of this early development is that different people may seek to work out the same predisposition in a variety of sociopolitical ways. For example, Erikson has argued that if a person acquires an early feeling of distrust, he may display cynicism toward politics and authority.[5] Yet it is also quite possible that such a person may continually search for a public leader in whom he can finally place his trust. The working out of psychological dispositions becomes a rather complex phenomenon to analyze with certainty.

To a large extent, researchers have chosen to identify psychological states and then relate them to aspects of political behavior that seem to correspond. This approach has considerable validity, yet it is necessary to remember that the individual personality operates within a rather structured political environment in which one's predispositions are not given free play. Because of this the child comes to realize that there are certain avenues of expressiveness which are socially acceptable. In this process the family is his central source of guidance.

The role of the family is itself an issue of considerable controversy and confusion. Generally, it seems that the family does not completely mold the personality of the child nor does it transmit very effectively its views on specific political and social questions. What the family does best is to transmit middle-range attitudes or predispositions on such topics as efficacy, involvement, information, partisanship, trust, and authority.

The predisposition which social scientists have concentrated on most, however, is that of authoritarianism. Adorno and his associates have found that "the presence or absence of extreme ethnic prejudice in individuals of our culture tends to be related to a complex network of attitudes, within, and relating to, the family."[6] This view has been reinforced by Lipset's analysis of authoritarian attitudes in the working classes of America and Europe. On the basis of a great deal of evidence, Lipset concluded that lower-class individuals are more likely to be exposed to punishment, lack of love, and a general atmosphere of tension and aggression. These experiences produce deep-rooted hostilities and lead to ethnic prejudice, political authoritarianism, and chiliastic transvaluational religion.[7]

These studies by social scientists emphasize the considerable relationships between childhood development and adult behavior patterns. Yet it is obvious that even though childhood may be a formative period, it is only one of many. While this period may be the most crucial one in a person's development, that development is not immune to the multitude of experiences that are characteristically a part of the entire life cycle.

At best then, the family can give to the child certain predispositions on topics like trust, efficacy, authority, tolerance, and other so-called political attitudes. In addition, the family also attempts to transmit moral attitudes which do have, or can have, political ramifications. The previous chapter explored some of these dimensions and their relationship to political socialization. However, one of the most important ways that children are inculcated into morality is through the mechanism of guilt. Its role is so important that it is necessary to examine its political dimensions separately.

Political Guilt

Guilt may be defined as "a special kind of negative self-evaluation which occurs when an individual acknowledges that his behavior is at variance with a given moral value to which he feels obligated to conform."[8] In Western cultures especially, guilt is one of the most important psychological mechanisms of social control. It becomes a watchdog which guards the standards of society within the individual's mind even when he seems to be alone.

Some psychologists maintain that fear of guilt is really the same as fear of external punishment. The child seeks to reward himself by imitating the parents' evaluative responses and he wishes to avoid even partial denial of their approval. In a simplified way, the individual feels guilty when he thinks that he is doing something which would imperil parental approval.[9]

In the socialization of their children, American parents, especially those in the middle class, rely on "love-oriented" techniques of discipline. Instead of physical punishment, these parents threaten to withdraw their affection if the child disobeys their commands. Such techniques tend to produce a very strong conscience and a high sense of guilt in children. In addition, because the identification process is so strong, the child frequently may absorb more items of social control than are really necessary.

The problem of inculcating moral values and guilt is very complex, more so than most parents realize. At one extreme, the child with too strong a conscience suffers from an excessive preoccupation with guilt and transgression. He avoids experimentation, becomes rigid, inflexible, sanctimonious, and incapable of experiencing even the little joys of life. At the other extreme is the child with a weak conscience who only fears getting caught and being punished. Such a child is very often mean, aggressive, and may even become criminal in his dealings with others.[10]

Historically, Americans have been cognizant of the importance of teaching moral values and of implanting feelings of guilt in their children. There are many different kinds of studies of child-rearing practices, but they generally show that middle-class Americans and Europeans, more than most other parents in the world, tend to exert severe pressures on the emotional development and bodily processes of their children. One of the best known studies is Whiting and Child's cross-cultural analysis which discovered that Americans are not at all indulgent with their infants. In fact, American parents are in a much greater hurry to train their children and are comparatively severe in their socialization methods. The authors conclude that the middle class in our society, and in the West generally, has a stronger average tendency toward guilt feelings than either the lower or upper classes. This fact becomes even more important when one realizes that middle-class parents also play a much more dominant role in the socialization process than do either lower- or upper-class parents.[11]

The only area where Americans are apparently a little less severe is in their treatment of aggression. It has been speculated that American parents are more tolerant of aggression because of the heavy emphasis which is placed on competition in our economic relationships. In fact, there is considerable evidence that child-rearing practices are, in part, due to the type of economy a society has. As the economy changes, the child-rearing practices change also. Sociologists have argued at length whether the achievement-oriented ideology of early capitalist America has given way to a more conformist and bureaucratic life-style. While it is difficult to answer that question for sure, it does seem that child-rearing practices have changed in the direction of the "love-oriented" techniques of the middle class.[12] Apparently then, the instilling of guilt is still an important part of the American socialization process and it is necessary, therefore, to assess its effects on the development of political attitudes.

Although Freud once called guilt "the most important problem in the evolution of culture," the topic itself has been relatively neglected. In the homeland of Hawthorne, Melville, and Faulkner, it should be obvious how many of our archetypal themes and political images betray the presence of extensive guilt feelings. A more contemporary example of political guilt is shown by the findings of the Kerner Commission on the civil disorders of 1968. The report is basically a white, middle-class indictment of white, middle-class America which ends with the remarkably candid conclusion that this is a racist society.[13]

The assassinations of the Kennedy brothers and of Dr. Martin Luther King brought forth a similar conclusion. American political and religious leaders debated for months whether we are comparatively a more violent and vicious people. Historians sought the root causes for these transgressions in our past; statisticians tallied up lists of our brutalities and compared them with other so-called civilized societies. Whether one agrees or disagrees with the conclusions and methodologies of the commissions on civil disorder and on violence, it is obvious that such conclusions could only have come from a leadership strata firmly imbued with the vocabulary and imagery of guilt. Perhaps the ultimate bankruptcy comes when all notions of guilt are "transcended" or bureaucraticized into operational rather than moral terms.[14]

Yet as pervasive as guilt is in the socialization process, it is quite difficult to explain aggregate behavior by referring to it. That the vocabulary of guilt is a part of our political dialogue is quite apparent, but to what extent does this vocalizing reflect itself in our actions?

It seems that like cynicism, for example, a feeling of guilt may lead to a variety of politically expressive avenues. First, guilt may be a genuine basis for social criticism and reconstruction. One example of this was the civil rights movement of the 1960s where blacks were joined by middle-class whites, many of whom were motivated by guilt and moral indignation. A second, alternative response to guilt-invoking situations is for the individual or group to deny that guilt is an appropriate feeling at all. A person may cite as a reason his own weakness, his distance in time or space from the debated events, or the fact that he was only obeying orders.

Lastly, one may engage in a widespread but little recognized defense: self-punishment. At first glance, it would seem that the logical outcome of social guilt would be to change the conditions that give rise to those feelings. Yet for many people the mere process of self-accusation can be sufficient enough "punishment" in and of itself. Thus the social utility of guilt is either sublimated, denied, or worn away.

This brief examination of guilt is by no means a comprehensive coverage of its relationship to politics, but it does show that still another aspect of the socialization process can affect the workings of the political system and the people in it. Americans are fond of thinking that the vocabulary or rhetoric of politics is devoid of meaning; whether we will admit it or not, people define themselves by the manner, the content, and the concerns which their words grope to explain. Guilt is one component of the psychopolitical drama as well as one of the mainstays of our system of moral feelings.

Partisan Affiliation

Political scientists have generally been less concerned with the transmittal of basic predispositions than they have been with specific and rather specialized political attitudes. One area that has received a great deal of attention is the important role that the family has in passing on its partisan affiliation. Children are more likely to "inherit" their party preference than they are to inherit any other social predisposition, except for religion.

In the United States, it has been found that "when the recalled party preference of both parents is the same, up to 80 percent of the respondents also report that preference."[15] The major study of American voting behavior breaks down the relationships in the ways shown in Table 3.1.

In addition, the family's influence on the stability of a voter's preferences increases when:

1. the party outlooks of its members are homogeneous
2. the political interest and loyalty among other members are high (this affects the direction of the preference more than the stability)
3. the same family preference has been retained over time
4. the life-styles (occupation, income, education, and religion) of the voter and his family are homogeneous.

Essentially, then, party identification is most likely to be transmitted when there are few competing influences to sway the voter. When there is disagreement between the family and other primary groups to which the voter belongs (e.g., spouse, friends), party irregularity and defection are more likely to occur. However, this situation does not happen as frequently as one might think. Most voters are "anchored in a matrix of politically harmonious primary associations—a result, to some extent, of conscious selection and of the tendency of the social environment to bring together people of like views."[16] Needless to say, the family plays a major role in this selection process and in interpreting that social environment.

The Family Power Structure

Some observers have indicated that the power structure of the family itself may have some effect on the political attitudes of children. One of the most interesting examinations of this dimension has been done by Kenneth P. Langton in his study of American and Jamaican secondary school students. He found that in both high authoritarian and low authoritarian families, party

Table 3.1
Intergenerational Resemblance in Partisan Orientation, Politically Active and Inactive Homes, 1958

Party identification of offspring	One or both parents were politically active			Neither parent was politically active	
	Both parents were Democrats	Both parents were Republicans	Parents had no consistent partisanship	Both parents were Democrats	Both parents were Republicans	Parents had no consistent partisanship
Strong Democrat	50%	5%	21%	40%	6%	20%
Weak Democrat	29	9	26	36	11	15
Independent	12	13	26	19	16	26
Weak Republican	6	34	16	3	42	20
Strong Republican	2	37	10	1	24	12
Apolitical	1	2	1	1	1	7
	100%	100%	100%	100%	100%	100%
Number of cases	333	194	135	308	187	199

Source: Angus Campbell, Philip Converse, Warren Miller, and Donald Stokes, *The American Voter*, p. 147, copyright © 1960 by John Wiley & Sons, Inc.

preference similarities were over 80 percent. Most of the partisan deviation occurred in the middle range. Apparently, democratic and highly authoritarian families manage, for different reasons, to hold on to their children's loyalties more than moderate families do.[17] The results of Langton's study are shown in Table 3.2.

When parents are very interested in politics, however, those who are authoritarian have a more difficult time in maintaining this pattern of consistency. Their children begin to reject their party label as they protest against domination in general. In less autocratic families, an increased interest in politics tends to strengthen partisan homogeneity between parents and children.[18] It appears that autocratic families are very effective only in transmitting affiliation when both the parents and the child are not highly politicized.

Another aspect of the family power structure is the effect which maternal dominance has on children. The general trend of social science research has been to stress the debilitating consequences of such dominance, especially on males. Langton's study supports this finding. Male students in his sample, regardless of class, were more likely to be authoritarian if they came from maternal families than if they came from nuclear families (those with both a father and a mother).

Children from maternal families also have less interest in politics except in the upper class where the inhibiting consequences are somewhat countered by other aspects of the political culture. The effects of class differences are also important in explaining political efficacy—there is a correlation between membership in maternal families and low political efficacy only in the lower class.

Table 3.2

Family Authoritarianism and Students' Deviance from Parents' Party Preference

Family Authoritarianism	Same as parents	Different from parents	Number of cases
High 1	83%	17%	125
2	62	38	230
3	71	29	537
Low 4	82	18	221

Source: From *Political Socialization* by Kenneth P. Langton, p. 26. Copyright © 1969 by Oxford University Press, Inc. Reprinted by permission.

Maternal families have no effect on males from the middle and upper classes in this study.

As for females, it appears that maternal dominance and paternal absence have little impact upon authoritarian attitudes and political interest. However, there is some indication that among working-class females, those who come from maternal families feel less efficacious than those from nuclear families.[19] In addition, it appears that the influence of the family power structure continues throughout high school; students from maternal families entered and left secondary school feeling less interested in politics, less efficacious, and more authoritarian than those from nuclear families.[20]

Even in nuclear families, when the mother is the dominant parent there still occurs a low sense of efficacy among males whose parents have a primary or secondary level education. However, in a family with college educated parents, maternal dominance encourages in a slight way, at least, male political involvement. The same pattern holds true when one looks at political interest. For the male child, at least, the effects of education and the power structure of his family are complex and crosscutting variables. As for the female child, there is little evidence that the variations in conjugal dominance had any effect on political attitudes.[21]

Maternal Influence

As is apparent, men are more interested and involved in politics than are women. Most of the early political socialization studies argued that men must also be more successful in transmitting their political attitudes to their children. While this assumption seems quite valid at first, it must be remembered that the mother is the most nurturant and important person in the lives of most children.

One study done by members of the Survery Research Center found that children of both sexes are more likely to get their political cues from their mother. This can be seen most clearly on the question of partisan affiliation. It seems that the mother exerts the predominant influence in transmitting partisanship. This influence can be measured in a variety of ways. First, in those instances where one parent belongs to one of the major parties and the other is an Independent, 39 percent of the children agree with the mother, 37 percent with the father, and 24 percent with neither. When one parent is a Democrat and the other is an Independent, a Democratic mother is more likely to pull children toward the party and less likely to lose them to the Republicans than when it is the father who is a Democrat. When one parent is a Republican and the other an Independent, a Republican mother is slightly more likely to pull children toward her party and less likely to lose them to the opposition party than when it is the father who is a Republican. (See Table 3.3.) In summary, it seems that the mother is a much more valuable asset for either party than is the father.[22]

A much stronger test of maternal dominance can be seen in the more pronounced splits—when one parent is a Democrat and the other is a Republican. Here too, the political influence of the mother is quite apparent, regardless of her partisan affiliation. When the mother is a Democrat, 44 percent of the offspring respondents acquired that label; when she is a Republican the plurality of the respondents again went over to her party. (See Table 3.4.) In the second situation, however, the ranks of the Independents swelled considerably. Probably, because of the usually Democratic national trends in our time, increased counter-pressures are applied to these respondents. Rather than either abandon the mother's party and join the other or buck these national political trends, students apparently choose the middle ground by avoiding a partisan label altogether. When voting pressures such as these occur it has been found that people usually attempt either to moderate somehow the demands placed on them or to avoid electoral politics.[23]

It is probable that this maternal dominance on the question of partisan affiliation is due to the greater emotional attachment and closer relationship mothers have with their children. In addition, the mother's influence increases at each educational level. Overall, the mother's influence moves from a 15 percent deficit vis-à-vis the father in families with a low level of education to a 12 percent advantage in the college educated families. This trend is even

Table 3.3

Relation between Party Identification of Parents and Offspring among Parents with a Partisan—Independent Party Identification Mix

Parental party identification mix		Student party identification				
Mother	Father	Demo-crat	Inde-pendent	Repub-lican	Total %	Number of cases
Democrat	Independent	51%	37%	12%	100	20
Independent	Democrat	39	40	21	100	20
Republican	Independent	21	34	45	100	14
Independent	Republican	43	17	40	100	15

Source: M. Kent Jennings and Kenneth P. Langton, "Mothers versus Fathers: The Formation of Political Orientations Among Young Americans," *Journal of Politics,* 31 (May 1969), p. 340.

Table 3.4
Relation between Party Identification of Bipolar Parents and Their Offspring

| Parental partisan identification mix || Student party identification ||| Total % | Number of cases |
Mother	Father	Democrat	Independent	Republican		
Democrat	Republican	44%	21%	35%	100	37
Republican	Democrat	29	38	33	100	23

Source: M. Kent Jennings and Kenneth P. Langton, "Mothers versus Fathers: The Formation of Political Orientations Among Young Americans," *Journal of Politics*, 31 (May 1969), p. 341.

more apparent when each of the parents belongs to a different party. In that situation the mother's influence moves from a 15 percent advantage in families with a low level of education to a 26 percent advantage in college educated families. It is logical to expect then that the increasing educational attainments of American women will not only accelerate their levels of political interest and information but will also solidify even further their dominance in this area.[24]

There is some evidence that this is happening already in families that are very involved in politics. As might be expected, children are more likely to be influenced by the parent who is intensely involved than by the one who is relatively less concerned. However, the mother in this case is the more powerful influence also. When she is the more intensely involved parent, there is a 27 percent difference in mother-father preference in her favor. When the father is the more intensely involved, he is more influential but only by 17 percent. The main investigators of this relationship, Jennings and Langton, have concluded that "when her activity and intensity levels increase the mother becomes a much more visible and salient source of political information."[25]

Of course, there are other topics which must be looked at besides partisan affiliation. Jennings and Langton also measured maternal dominance on value orientations and again they found that there was a higher percentage of agreement with the mother than with the father. There appears then to be little evidence to support the notion that children receive more of their political cues and issue orientations from their father. Once again it seems obvious that as women become more educated, more independent, and more politicized their total political influence on their offspring will become accentuated.[26]

Maternal Influence

Recruitment

Another area in which the family also plays a major role is in transmitting to its children a sense of political interest and efficacy. It is by no means "natural" that people come to be intensely interested in politics and willing to participate in its processes. The child's level of information, degree of interest, and his willingness to participate are all influenced by the family's own inclinations in these areas. As will be seen later, the socioeconomic level at which a family exists also contributes, to some extent, to a child's desire to listen to and later engage in political dialogue and activities.

In the United States, the leadership or political recruitment process is heavily influenced by the family's early socialization practices. Studies vary but generally it has been found that the proportion of politically active leaders who trace their involvement to parental influence ranges between 30 and 40 percent. In one study of political recruitment done by Kenneth Prewitt, half of the leaders explained their interest in politics by mentioning the political socialization process in one way or another.[27] Both the school and the family were important agents in their development.

These leaders, whose interest in politics stems from childhood socialization experience, tend to adopt a partisan rather than a civic role more frequently than those leaders who are recruited later into public life. (See Table 3.5.) In addition, these leaders are more likely to be motivated by a simple

Table 3.5

Attitudes Associated with Initial Activity Related to the Three Entry Patterns

	Politically socialized	Politically mobilized	Lateral entrants	Totals
Sense of indignation	16%	18%	15%	17%
Feeling of obligation	7	10	17	10
Pragmatism orientation	20	21	2	18
General interest	25	16	6	19
Miscellaneous	3	1	0	2
No attitude mentioned	29	33	59	34
	100%	100%	100%	100%
Number of cases	214	163	54	431

Source: From *The Recruitment of Political Leaders: A Study of Citizen-Politicians* by Kenneth Prewitt, copyright © 1970, by The Bobbs-Merrill Company, Inc., reprinted by permission of the publisher.

interest in politics than by a feeling of personal obligation. For them, politics has become a natural area in which to be interested and concerned.[28]

There are other patterns of political recruitment which are less established than these traditional middle-class pathways. One of the most interesting topics of leadership studies is how and why so-called nonadaptable types enter politics. Are such leaders motivated by "psychopathic" backgrounds, by status anxiety, by sheer opportunism? Or are they marginal men who, because of their moral background and insights, are more willing to challenge society's pretensions?[29] We know little about the motivations of such nonadaptable leaders and even less about the origins of their motivations. What effect the early political socialization process has on them is rather unclear. However, it is apparent that at least among the traditional American leadership strata, the family plays an important role in sensitizing its young to the value of political information, the worth of personal effort, and the honor of public office.

Transmitting Issue Attitudes

The last area which must be considered is the extent to which the family passes on its attitudes on specific political issues. In looking at the belief systems of the public, it is quite obvious that for most people politics is not a primary concern. The level of information among the populace is generally rather low. In addition, there is often little correlation between one's commitment to general abstract principles and the willingness and/or conceptual ability to apply them to specific judgments. For example, while a large majority of the populace claims to believe in freedom of speech, nearly half are unwilling to allow those whom they passionately disagree with to exercise that freedom.[30]

The belief systems of the public are not coherent nor are they based on a very high level of information. It is rather unlikely that there is much concerted and intelligent family conversation on political issues or even personalities.[31] One would assume, however, that the family was at least somewhat effective in passing on its attitudes toward groups. Yet one major study has indicated that this is not necessarily so. Table 3.6 shows that while the aggregate scores are rather similar, the actual correlations between a student's views and those of his parents are strikingly low.

In addition, on the specific issues of integration, school prayer, and freedom of speech, the correlations were low or insignificant. These correlations were low regardless of whether or not a student came from a highly politicized background. Thus the role of the family in transmitting its specific

Table 3.6

Correlations between Parent–Student Group Evaluations

Group evaluated	Parent–student correlations	Mean ratings Parent	Mean ratings Student
Catholics	.36	72	70
Southerners	.30	66	62
Labor unions	.28	60	60
Negroes	.26	67	69
Jews	.22	67	63
Whites	.19	84	83
Protestants	.15	84	79
Big business	.12	64	63

Source: M. Kent Jennings and Richard G. Niemi, "The Transmission of Political Values from Parent to Child," *American Political Science Review,* 62 (March 1968), p. 176.

issue or group attitudes is quite limited. Obviously this influence becomes even less pervasive as the child matures and moves into the larger political environment.[32]

Summary

The role of the family in the political socialization process is important, but it is not all-embracing. Overall, the family's influence is most apparent at the middle-range level of attitudes. As we have seen, the family does not mold the child's total personality and fix his early attitudes forever; nor does it transmit very effectively its specific judgments on issues or groups. However, the family does lay the early foundations of partisanship, efficacy, self-esteem, information, trust, and morality.

Lastly, the family is important in one other major way as well: it is located within a certain socioeconomic framework which has some effect on the child's political development. By its very location in time and society, the family is placing the child in a series of learning situations which have direct consequences for political socialization.

Notes

1. Irving L. Janis, George F. Mahl, Jerome Kagan, and Robert R. Holt, *Personality: Dynamics, Development, and Assessment* (New York: Harcourt, Brace & World, 1969), p. 444.

2. The family's role is examined in Stephen L. Wasby, "The Impact of the Family on Politics: An Essay and Review of the Literature," *The Family Life Coordinator*, 15 (1966), 3–23 and John C. Davies, "The Family's Role in Political Socialization," *The Annals*, 361 (September 1965), 10–19. An older analysis is given in Sarah Carolyn Fisher, *Relationships in Attitudes, Opinions, and Values Among Family Members* (Berkeley: University of California Press, 1948). Also of use are Talcott Parsons and Robert F. Bales, *Family: Socialization and Interaction Process* (Glencoe, Ill.: Free Press, 1955); David B. Lynn and William L. Sawrey, "The Effects of Father Absence on Norwegian Boys and Girls," *Journal of Abnormal and Social Psychology*, 59 (1959), 258–262; and Robert A. Levine, "The Role of the Family in Authority Systems: A Cross Cultural Application of Stimulus-Generalization Theory," *Behavioral Science*, 5 (October 1960), 291–297.

3. Albert Bandura and Richard Walters, *Social Learning and Personality Development* (New York: Holt, 1963); Bandura, D. Ross, and S. A. Ross, "Transmission of Aggression through Imitation of Aggressive Models," *Journal of Abnormal and Social Psychology*, 63 (1961), 575–582; Bandura and F. G. MacDonald, "The Influence of Social Reinforcement and Behavior of Models in Shaping Children's Moral Judgments," *Journal of Abnormal and Social Psychology*, 67 (1963), 274–281; and Bandura and A. Huston, "Identification as a Process of Incidental Learning," *Journal of Abnormal and Social Psychology*, 63 (1961), 311–318. The role of aggressive models is discussed in Boyd McCandless, "Childhood Socialization," *Handbook of Socialization Theory and Research*, edited by David A. Goslin (Chicago: Rand McNally, 1969), pp. 791–820.

4. A concise overview of personality can be found in Lawrence A. Pervin, *Personality: Theory, Assessment and Research* (New York: Wiley, 1970), chap. 1 and in John A. Clausen and Judith R. Williams, "Sociological Correlates of Child Behavior," *Child Development*, edited by Harold W. Stevenson (Chicago: University of Chicago Press, 1963), pp. 791–820.

5. As noted in the previous chapter, Erikson's concept of trust is developed most thoroughly in his *Identity: Youth and Crisis* (New York: Norton, 1968) and *Childhood and Society* (New York: Norton, 1950).

6. T. W. Adorno, Else Frenkel-Brunswik, Daniel J. Levinson, and R. N. Sanford, *The Authoritarian Personality* (New York: Harper, 1950), p. 384. The topic is explored in many other sources, including Milton Rokeach, *The Open and Closed Mind* (New York: Basic Books, 1960); Richard Christie and Peggy Cook, "A Guide to Published Literature Relating to the Authoritarian Personality through 1956," *Journal of Psychology*, 45 (1958), 171–199; F. Samelson and J. F. Yates, "Acquiescence and the F Scale: Old Assumptions and the New Data," *Psychological Bulletin*, 68 (1967), 91–103; and Morris Janowitz and Dwaine Marvick, "Authoritarianism and Political Behavior," *Public Opinion Quarterly*, 17 (Summer 1953), 185–201. Morris Rosenberg argues that personal trust and political trust are related in "Misanthropy and Political Ideology," *American Sociological Review*, 21 (December 1956), 690–695.

7. S. M. Lipset, *Political Man* (New York: Anchor Books, 1960), p. 114. For

an interesting critique of this line of thought see Michael P. Rogin, *McCarthy and the Intellectuals* (Cambridge, Mass.: MIT Press, 1971).

8. David P. Ausubel, "Relationships between Shame and Guilt in the Socialization Process," *Psychological Review*, 62 (1955), 379. Some useful comparisons are drawn in Robert Ginder and Robert McMichael, "Cultural Influences on Conscience Developments: Resistance to Temptation and Guilt among Samoans and American Caucasians," *Journal of Abnormal and Social Psychology*, 66 (1963), 503–507.

9. John W. M. Whiting and Irving Child, *Child Training and Personality* (New Haven, Conn.: Yale University Press, 1953), pp. 233, 317. The concept of guilt has been discussed at length by Justin Aronfreed, *Conduct and Conscience* (New York: Academic, 1968) and in his "The Nature, Variety and Social Patterning of Moral Responses to Transgression," *Journal of Abnormal and Social Psychology*, 63 (1961), 223–241.

10. Robert R. Sears, Eleanor E. Maccoby and Harry Lewis, *Patterns of Child Rearing* (Evanston, Ill.: Row, Peterson, 1957), pp. 389–392 and Althea H. Stein, "Imitation of Resistance to Temptation," *Child Development*, 38 (1967), 167.

11. Whiting and Child, *Child Training and Personality*, p. 320.

12. Two of the best known discussions of the nature of American economic life and its effects on child-rearing patterns are David Reisman, Nathan Glazer, and Reuel Denny, *The Lonely Crowd* (New Haven, Conn.: Yale University Press, 1950) and David C. McClelland, *The Achieving Society* (Princeton: Van Nostrand, 1961). A fascinating anthropological study is Herbert A. Barry, Irwin L. Child, and Margaret K. Bacon, "Relation of Child-Training to Subsistence Economy," *American Anthropologist*, 61 (February 1969), 51–63.

13. *The Report of the National Advisory Commission on Civil Disorders* (New York: Bantam, 1968) and Hugh D. Graham and Ted Robert Gurr, *The History of Violence in America* (New York: Bantam, 1970).

14. One of the few good anthologies on the topic of political guilt is Roger W. Smith, *Guilt: Man and Society* (New York: Anchor Books, 1971). The bureaucratic transcendance of guilt is best explained in Hannah Arendt, *Eichmann in Jerusalem: A Report on the Banality of Evil* (New York: Viking, 1964) and can be seen also in the New York Times summary of *The Pentagon Papers* (New York: Bantam, 1971).

15. Kenneth Langton, *Political Socialization* (New York: Oxford University Press, 1969), p. 53.

16. Herbert McCloskey and Harold E. Dahlgreen, "Primary Group Influence and Party Loyalty," *American Political Science Review*, 53 (September 1959), 757–776.

17. Langton, *Political Socialization*, p. 26. Other examinations of the family power structure are John A. Clausen, "Family Structure, Socialization and Personality," *Review of Child Development Research*, Vol. 2, edited by L. W. Hoffman and Martin Hoffman (New York: Russell Sage Foundation, 1966), pp. 1–54; Murray A. Straus, "Power and Support Structure of the Family in Relation to Socialization," *Journal of Marriage and the Family*, 26 (1964), 318–326; and Straus, "Conjugal Power Structure and Adolescent Personality," *Marriage and Family Living*, 24 (1962), 17–25.

18. Langton, *Political Socialization*, p. 29.

19. Langton, pp. 36–38.

20. Langton, p. 42.

21. Langton, pp. 48–51.

22. M. Kent Jennings and Kenneth Langton, "Mothers verses Fathers: The Formation of Political Orientations among Young Americans," *Journal of Politics*, 31 (May 1969), 339–340.

23. Jennings and Langton, p. 340. Also see Richard M. Merleman, "Intimate Environments and Political Behavior," *Midwest Journal of Political Science*, 12 (August 1968), 382–400.

24. Merleman, p. 344.

25. Merleman, p. 346.

26. Merleman, p. 357. There does appear to be some weakening of partisan affiliations which can be seen in the noticeable rise in the number of young people who term themselves Independents. This is somewhat apparent in M. Kent Jennings and Richard G. Niemi, "The Transmission of Political Values from Parent to Child," *American Political Science Review*, 62 (March 1968), 173.

27. Kenneth Prewitt, *The Recruitment of Political Leaders: A Study of Citizen-Politicians* (Indianapolis: Bobbs-Merrill, 1971), p. 65. His first chapters cite nearly all the major references on this topic. For evidence that the development of political efficacy is more heavily dependent on the family than on other factors, see Prewitt and P. A. Karns, "The Relative Influence of the Family, Peer Group, and the School in the Development of Political Efficacy," *Western Political Quarterly*, 22 (December 1969), 813–826.

28. Prewitt, pp. 88–89, 97. Other evidence of recruitment practices is in Prewitt and Heinz Eulau, "Social Bias in Leadership Selection, Political Recruitment and Electoral Context," *Journal of Politics*, 33 (May 1971), 293–315; D. C. Schwartz, "Towards a Theory of Political Recruitment," *Western Political Quarterly*, 22 (September 1969), 552–571. Norman H. Nie, G. P. Powell, Jr., and Kenneth Prewitt, "Social Structure and Political Participation," *American Political Science Review*, 63 (June 1969), 361–378 and (September 1969), 808–832; R. R. Alford and H. H. Scoble, "Sources of Local Political Involvement," *American Political Science Review*, 62 (December 1968), 1192–1206; and Roderick Bell, "The Determinants of Psychological Involvement in Politics: A Causal Analysis," *Midwest Journal of Political Science*, 13 (May 1969), 237–253.

29. G. E. Marcus, "Psychopathology and Political Recruitment," *Journal of Politics*, 31 (November 1969), 913–931; Harold Lasswell, *Power and Personality* (New York: Viking, 1948); and Richard Hofstadter, *The Paranoid Style of American Politics* (New York: Knopf, 1960).

30. Herbert McClosky, "Consensus and Ideology in American Politics," *American Political Science Review*, 58 (June 1964), 361–382; and James W. Prothro and Charles W. Grigg, "Fundamental Principles of Democracy: Bases of Agreement and Disagreement," *Journal of Politics*, 22 (May 1960), 276–294.

31. The best discussion of popular beliefs is Philip E. Converse, "The Nature of Belief Systems in Mass Publics," *Ideology and Discontent*, edited by David E. Apter (Glencoe, Ill.: Free Press, 1964), 206–261. For evidence that voters have become more issue oriented since the election of 1964 see Gerald M. Pomper, "From Confusion to Clarity: Issues and American Voters, 1956–1968," *American Political Science Review*, 66 (June 1972), 415–428.

32. Jennings and Niemi, "The Transmission of Political Values," 172–176. This sample was done with secondary school seniors and their parents.

four

The Social Nexus
Sex, Class, Peers, and Ethnicity

The last two chapters have stressed the common aspects of the socialization process during the latent stages of political development. However, even during these stages the child's learning is already being affected by many variables. This chapter examines four of the most important of these: sex, class, peer groups, and ethnic background.

Sex Differences

It may seem incorrect to treat a biological difference as a social factor, but researchers have come to recognize the difficulty in trying to sort out the social aspects of sex-role behavior and the specific genetic differences between male and female. Indeed, before a child knows what the actual biological difference is, he or she is already immersed in the conventional patterns of appropriate sex-role behavior. Toys, dress, length of hair, degree of cleanliness, and level of aggressiveness all become part of this early and quite subtle process of role differentiation.[1]

This differentiation is important because it applies to politics as well. In the United States, politics is seen as an activity or a "sport" that is more appropriate for men than for women. It need not be so; there are records of many matriarchal societies where women were the dominant sex in political decision making. But in this country, and in nearly the whole modern world, the proportion of women in public life is infinitesimal.[2]

There is then an early categorization of people into sexual roles which has an effect on political behavior. The previous chapter noted one such instance: the apparently superior influence of the mother in transmitting political values to her children. Such superiority is undoubtedly due to her early activities as the most nurturant parent in the child's life. But most studies on sex differences and political behavior play down the importance of the female's role. The French political scientist, Maurice Duverger, has gone so far as to indicate that while "women have, legally, ceased to be minors, they still have the mentality of minors in many fields and, particularly in politics, they usually accept paternalism on the part of men. The man—husband, fiancé, lover, or myth—is the mediator between them and the political world."[3]

However satisfying that observation may be to the male reader, sex differences in political behavior are much more complicated in modern America. For example, one of the best documented differences is in the area of voting; women have about a 10 percent lower turnout rate than do men. But even this difference is subject to qualification. First, as one investigates voting turnout among the better educated, these differences level out considerably. Also, it appears that one of the major reasons for the lower female turnout is simply that domestic responsibilities, especially child care, makes it more difficult for women to vote. Campbell and his associates found that among "younger people who are single or married without children ... there is little or no 'average difference' in turnout between men and women across categories of education and age outside the South."[4] However, for older women and those living in less cosmopolitan regions, it does appear that traditional concepts of sex-role behavior still curtail political activity.

Campbell and his associates also found that men and women tend to approach politics in different ways. First, women are somewhat less likely to express a sense of involvement in politics than are men, although among college graduates this difference is obliterated or even reversed. Second, while both sexes have the same sense of civic responsibility, women are less likely to feel politically efficacious even when education, age, and income are controlled. This finding has led Campbell and his associates to conclude "that moralistic values about citizen participation in democratic government have been bred in women as in men; what has been less adequately transmitted to the woman is a sense of some personal competence vis-à-vis the political world."[5]

Women are also much less sophisticated in their conceptualization of issues and they often inflate the "no opinion" and "no information" response categories in attitude surveys. Generally, they are much less likely to be issue oriented than men even when they have the same educational background;

women tend more often to make their political judgments on the simpler basis of whether the times are good or bad and whether the social groups to which they belong are benefiting from government policies.[6] (See Table 4.1.)

Other studies have pointed up the fact that women are less willing to support aggressive policies, are less tolerant of nonconformity, and are more concerned with local rather than with national issues. In addition, Greenstein has argued that women are more likely to support sumptuary legislation—for example, restrictions on alcohol consumption and gambling.[7]

These attitude differences between the sexes are present in young children as well. Most of the early studies indicate that boys are more knowledgeable about and more interested in politics. In his sample of New Haven students, Greenstein found additional evidence to support this view. (See Table 4.2) Overall, wherever the questionnaire that he used differentiated between boys and girls, the former were almost always found to be more "political." Even as early as fourth grade, boys were more informed, more able to name partisan leaders, more likely to advocate political change, and more interested in political information.[8]

It is apparent then that appropriate sex-role behavior plays an important part in mediating between the child and the political world. Because politics is considered a masculine activity, male interest is heightened, and feelings of efficacy and saliency are accentuated. For the female citizen, the opposite occurs with obvious results. To a large extent then, in the socialization of sexual roles, adults have very often socialized their children into active and passive political roles as well. However, in the long-run these differences will become minimal as the educational level of women rises.

Table 4.1
Relation of Sex and Education to Level of Conceptualization, 1956

Level of conceptualization	Grade school Male	Grade school Female	High school Male	High school Female	College Male	College Female
A. Ideology	8%	1%	17%	5%	34%	27%
B. Group benefit	43	33	52	44	36	34
C. Nature of times	30	26	19	26	19	21
D. No issue content	19	40	12	25	11	18
	100%	100%	100%	100%	100%	100%
Number of cases	251	291	354	537	175	155

Source: Angus Campbell, et. al., *The American Voter*, p. 491, copyright © 1960 by John Wiley & Sons, Inc.

Table 4.2

Sex Differences in Political Responses: Fourth Graders and Total New Haven Sample

Questionnaire items	Fourth grade subsample Boys	Fourth grade subsample Girls	Total sample (grades 4-8) Boys	Total sample (grades 4-8) Girls
Specifically political responses				
Political information score	3.30	2.77†	4.69	4.31*
Can name at least one party leader	41%	33%	56%	48%
Proposes "political" change in the world	13	5	41	34
Will vote when twenty-one years old	76	77	80	81
Believes "elections are important"	69	72	72	73
Politically relevant responses				
Names interesting news story	65	47	73	60*
Story named is political	15	12	36	12*
Names pleasant news story	39	28	54	41*
Story named is political	9	2	26	17*
Names unpleasant news story	37	35	53	43†
Story named is political	18	9	33	20*
Prefers Washington to New Haven news	52	35	38	26*
Names someone from public life as "famous person you want to be like"	39	23	24	15
Names someone from public life as "famous person you *don't* want to be like"	22	14	32	13*
Number of cases	54	57	337	332

*A sex difference is significant at the 1 percent level.
†A sex difference is significant at the 5 percent level.

Source: Fred I. Greenstein, *Children and Politics* (New Haven: Yale University Press, 1965), p. 117. Previously published in Fred I. Greenstein, "Sex-Related Political Differences in Childhood," *Journal of Politics,* 23 (May 1961), p. 361.

The Consequences of Class

Like sex-role differentiation, the effects of class in the socialization process are much more complex than is at first apparent. One problem is that in the United States it is very difficult to define with even moderate precision the unique characteristics of each socioeconomic group. This is not to say that classes do not exist. They do and the maldistribution of personal and corporate wealth is one visible testimony of the extent of structural inequities. But for the purposes of this study it must be proven that this stratification has consequences for the political socialization process.

One of the most frequently examined aspects of class differences is in the area of child-rearing practices. For a considerable period of time, child psychologists maintained that there were important variations in the way lower-class and middle-class parents raised their offspring. Lower-class parents were more concerned with physical discipline and conformity while middle-class parents resorted to reasoning, persuasion, and the threat of withdrawing their love to control children. In addition, while middle-class parents can be somewhat severe in their subtle socialization practices, they also seem to be more tolerant of differences of opinion and generally more democratic in the management of family affairs.

As we have seen in the previous chapters, some researchers have stressed that these so-called nonpolitical aspects of family life have consequences for the way children come to view authority and power relationships. Lipset, for example, has indicated that one of the main causes for the high rate of authoritarianism among working-class families is the type of child-rearing practices that are employed.[9]

In addition, many studies have found that the levels of information, participation, and efficacy are weaker among lower-class adults than among members of the other two classes. After examining these differences, Robert Lane has put forth several explanations for the influence of socioeconomic status upon political activity. He maintains that lower status persons lack economic security and feel less sense of control over their political environment. Lower status people are less likely than upper status people to see that the politics of the modern welfare state can offer them immediate and visible benefits. They also tend to withdraw from social contact with mixed groups, are more deferential toward others, and generally exhibit little self-confidence. The result is that lower status people deemphasize participation and civic involvement. Politics becomes a chore to them; they belong to few groups, feel more cross pressured by others, and are less able to deal with abstract issues.[10]

There are, of course, some factors which tend to offset these disadvantages. Interclass social mobility, membership in quasipolitical organizations (such as labor unions), or even an articulate populist leader can overcome, but not totally compensate for, these psychological differences. But the present patterns of political participation tend to support Lane's analysis. People from lower status groups (or classes, to use a less precise term) are caught in a web of expectations, observations, and reinforcements that have the cumulative effect of denigrating participatory citizenship.

In his examination of political socialization in New Haven, Greenstein maintained that the effects of class differences were present among children as well. He found that higher status children possessed superior verbal and scholastic capacity as well as greater intellectual and psychic autonomy. Upper status children had more of a capacity and motivation for participation and they were better able to distinguish between the parties and name leaders than were lower status children.[11]

In addition, children from upper status groups were more likely to respond in political terms when asked how to change the world and also were more willing to classify themselves as Independents. While nearly all young children tend to idealize authority figures, it seems that upper status children are more likely to take a realistic view of politics earlier in life.

One of the most surprising findings in the New Haven sample is that both status groups had the same amount of information on how government institutions work. In contrast to adult behavior patterns, there was no difference between the groups on the questions of whether one should vote and whether elections are important. Apparently the school is a very significant leveling force in this area.[12]

Peer Groups

The socioeconomic status of a family has another effect: it places the child within a framework of relationships where he is educated, acquires skills, and makes friends. The influence of the last factor is rather significant for both children and adults. In Chapter 2 it was pointed out that the child begins to be affected by his peer group playmates even during the latent phases of political socialization. Decisions are made and games are played by rules commonly accepted and agreed upon. In this way, children come to realize very early in life the importance of collective action.

In the early phases of a child's preschool development, the role of the peer group appears to be minimal. But soon the child enters into the world of organized play and then into the formal environment of the school. He begins to respect the judgment of his peers and desires to be popular with them. Thus the peer group becomes a circle of equals within which a person asserts or humiliates himself.

By the time the child reaches the "juvenile era" or prepubescent period, the peer group becomes an important supplement to the family in the socialization process.[13] It is really only during adolescence, however, that the peer group emerges as a paramount factor in personality development. Even the most casual observer can see that the peer group is an important social reference for the adolescent. To a large extent, the trials and tribulations of growing up, acquiring an identity, and learning to work with and feel for others are all dependent on peer group activities.

Despite—or perhaps because of—all this, politics does not really command much of the energies of adolescents. It is true that the unbalancing effects of this period of physiological and psychological maturation can lead to an extreme altruism or a desire for a sort of personal martyrdom. But for the vast majority of adolescents, politics is not a very salient long-term concern. For example, when the Purdue Opinion Polls were completed in the 1950s they showed that teenagers were worried about personal problems, even to the total exclusion of social issues.[14] A later study done by James S. Coleman does not even deal with political issues. This neglect may represent a serious oversight on the part of an otherwise superb study, or, more likely, it may simply be that the adolescent world is one totally circumscribed by dating, athletics, and the search for social recognition.[15]

While the adolescent is going through this period of stress, it is obvious that he is likely to come in conflict with his parents. Many people have postulated that there even occurs a dramatic generational split in which the younger members of society break with traditional values and reject parental influence. The implications for political socialization are obvious: if such a break does occur, then the role of the family diminishes as that of the peer group is placed in ascendency.

Some critics have even gone so far as to argue that adolescent peer groups are dangerous because they promote antisocial behavior and tend to work at cross pressures with adult institutions. One of the most interesting observations in this regard comes from Urie Bronfenbrenner. In his study of American and Russian children, Bronfenbrenner found that while Soviet peer groups reinforce the adult value system, American peer groups try to create a world in which the adolescent can either lament the loss of his childhood or seek refuge from the demands of adult society.[16]

Despite the considerable publicity about a generation gap, there is really little evidence that American adolescents reject the basic value system of their parents. Douvan and Adelson maintain that adolescent value ferment is usually due to intrapsychic conflict more than to anything else. They also found that whatever adolescent rebellion there is, it exhausts itself on tastes and manners rather than on value differences. In fact, by accentuating the former concerns, the conflict which does occur is actually a "psuedo-rebellion" which stops at the threshold of basic values.[17]

However, for a very small group of adolescents, some genuine value change does take place and it is this group that often becomes the elite that sets the tone for the whole generation. Interestingly enough, the members of this elite usually come from liberal backgrounds and have the strong (even if silent) support of like-minded peer or adult models in their search for a new value system.[18]

Actually, some measure of conflict may be beneficial. When the family and the peer group have the same values, it is very unlikely that a person will deviate far from his original training. Douvan and Adelson have argued that children in this situation are docile, bland, and morally and ideologically parochial. One can often see this happening with children from isolated rural areas or self-contained subcultures.[19]

There are few major studies on family-peer group political conflict. Two older studies, one done at Cornell and the other at Bennington, lend some credence to the idea that when politics does become important, peer group or prestige group influence can be decisive.[20] Also, the McCarthy and McGovern movements and the student strike of May 1969 (protesting Nixon's invasion of Cambodia) are good examples of peer group influence which mobilized large segments of college youth into political channels.

Most of the evidence that we have indicates that, despite intergenerational differences, adolescents still have a great respect for their parents' views. While Coleman found that students fear displeasing their peers more than their parents, many other studies point to the opposite conclusion. Remmers and Radler concluded that teenagers in their sample were more sensitive to the feelings of their parents and other adults on political questions than they are to peer group opinions. In another study, Epperson found an 80 percent level of agreement between students and their parents. A sample of Jewish adolescents—normally one of the most politically radical groups—found that when they were asked to name persons whose opinions mattered a great deal, over 90 percent named one or both parents and in almost all cases they named them first.[21]

Other studies have found that students are more likely to disagree with their parents on political matters when they are emotionally estranged or when family ties are weak. This finding can be supplemented with Langton's observation that children from maternal families are more likely to seek political advice and to be influenced by outsiders (including peer groups) than those from nuclear families. In addition, Langton points up another complication: peer groups are not necessarily homogeneous in their makeup. Children, as well as adults, realize that there are subordinate and superordinate statuses in groups. Higher status peers become important as models for imitation and they bestow on their followers approval, attention, and even leadership roles. In heterogeneous peer groups, working-class members tend to be resocialized toward the level of politicization and political outlook of the upper-class members.[22]

Overall, however, youth peer groups do not substantially change the basic, deep-rooted values instilled in children by their parents. This is usually due to the fact that the social backgrounds and values of the family and the peer groups are usually so similar. When they are different, the influence of the family is dependent upon how strong its affective ties are with its children.[23]

It is also important to realize that peer group influence, whatever its strength, does not cease at adolescence. Peer groups are also important in explaining adult behavior. The voluminous amount of literature on reference groups and voting indicates that many people are strongly influenced by their friends and coworkers. It is difficult to assess the specific importance of reference groups because, once again, members often share a common background, come from the same socioeconomic status, and have similar interests.[24]

One of the apparent examples of how peer group influences can shape political behavior is found in the study of political elites. The major works on legislative behavior, especially on Congressional committees, heavily emphasize the ways in which elected officials are socialized into certain patterns of role behavior. They are, in a sense, inculcated into certain career channels in which the process of occupational socialization is reinforced by rewards, punishments, and general feelings of rejection and acceptance.[25]

The Ethnic Factor

Despite the obvious importance of ethnic groups in American life, there are really few good studies on the subject. The term *ethnic group* is even less precise than the terms *class* or *peer group* which we have used rather loosely before. The most comprehensive definition of ethnicity would include religious, racial, national, and cultural groups. The major ethnic groups that are usually cited are: Jews, Catholics, blacks, and nationality groups, such as Irish, Polish, German, and Italian Americans. Many more could easily be added to the list.

If ethnic groups, with all their significance, have never been systematically analyzed, it is not surprising that little is known or even speculated about the effects of ethnic background on the political socialization process.[26] It has generally been assumed that white Protestant groups such as the English, Scandanavians, and even Germans had little difficulty in accepting the core culture of America. Yet even these groups developed very different styles of political behavior. Swedish Americans, for example, generally had little interest in politics, while Norwegian Americans were steadfast Republicans and important defenders of the agrarian way of life. In contrast, many Finnish Americans and some German Americans were rather receptive to socialist movements, especially at the beginning of this century.[27]

This variety of political views was even more pronounced in the second wave of immigrants, most of whom were Catholic. Irish, Italian, Polish, and Slavic Americans were less easily assimilated, but sooner or later they and their descendents came to accept the core culture.[28] One of the main reasons why there has been so little examination of ethnicity is that it has been assumed that by the third generation all of these group differences would disappear under the pressures of assimiliation. A second reason is that intermarriage, especially within white Protestant groups and within Catholic groups, has created a unique sort of melting pot effect in which national ethnicity has been replaced by religion as the major characteristic difference between the various groups. Thus while one may seek to examine the diverse socialization practices of Irish Americans or Italian Americans, by this time in history it might be more profitable to examine instead the attitudes of second- and third-generation Catholic Americans.[29]

Almost all studies of white ethnic groups end up with a commentary on how successful American assimiliation has been. Yet some important exceptions to this general observation do remain. Many groups have isolated themselves either through choice or because of outside compulsion and therefore exhibit different life-styles and political behavior. This is most obvious in certain religious groups or communities such as the Amish, Jehovah Witnesses, and to some extent, Mormons.

There has been a recent growth of political consciousness among many groups, including blacks, Chicanos, Puerto Ricans, Indians, Oriental Americans, and even, to a lesser degree, white ethnic groups as well. Such a reemergence of cultural identity is bound to have some impact on political behavior and on the attitudes which children have toward the core culture and its presuppositions on government. As of yet, however, there is little evidence as to what effect differences in ethnic background have on the political socialization process.

There are, however, three major ethnic groups that have been investigated in some depth—Catholics, Jews, and blacks. While Catholics are more numerous and probably the most varied in their background characteristics, there are some marked differences between Catholics as a group and the rest of the population. For example, every voting study has pointed out that Catholics, even when class is controlled for, are more likely to vote Democratic than are white Protestants. This affiliation may be an accidental biproduct of the patterns of early immigration and the inheritance of party preference from then on; or it may be that religious affiliation actually influences party affiliation.[30]

There are some other important differences among religious groups. One study found that white Protestants are more likely to favor nonpartisan elections and to deemphasize the importance of social conflict than are either Catholics or black Protestants. White Protestants are also less likely to approve of government intervention in the economy than are Catholics or blacks. Overall then, white Protestants are more conservative on economic issues but more tolerant of civil liberties than are Catholics.[31] Probably some of the effects of class background have influenced these findings even after class has been "controlled." It may be that working-class attitudes are so interwoven into the belief systems of Catholic Americans that even though they leave the lower class, their views continue to be influenced by the experiences of the past.

Another important question is to what extent do Catholic parochial schools inculcate in their nearly 6 million pupils values that are different on the topic of citizenship and political responsibility. The best study on the subject, done by Greeley and Rossi, indicates that while Catholics as a group are more conservative on civil liberties, for example, this attitude is not necessarily linked to parochial schools. In fact, there is evidence that Catholic adults who are educated in Catholic schools are somewhat more tolerant on civil liberties than are their co-religionists educated in public schools. Also contrary to the popular sterotype, Catholic college graduates from Catholic institutions are less likely to have racist and anti-Semitic attitudes than Protestant college graduates.[32] Thus it appears that while there are some differences between Catholics and Protestants, they are less apparent than is usually assumed.

A much easier ethnic group to deal with is the Jews. Nearly all the major studies done on Jewish American political behavior shows that despite their comparatively higher levels of education and income, middle-class Jews are more likely to support government intervention on economic issues than even working-class Catholics and Protestants. Also as a group, they are more likely to be "civic-minded," that is, to support public welfare proposals even if they do not directly benefit from them. Coupled with this economic liberalism, Jews have usually been very supportive of civil rights for minorities and quite sensitive to infringments on civil liberties. The major liberal movements of the 1960s dealing with race relations, poverty, and war were supported by substantial numbers of Jewish students and their parents—substantial in the sense that it was far out of proportion to their total strength of three percent of the population.[33]

It may be argued that the reasons for Jewish liberalism, especially on issues of civil liberties, are their higher education and income levels; both of these factors are characteristics of other liberal segments in society as well. However, it appears that civil libertarianism as well as economic liberalism are inculcated more strongly in Jewish children than in other children.* To a large extent, a form of liberal humanitarianism is a part of their basic religious temper. In general, then, the American Jewish community has played a major role in socializing its children into a markedly more liberal and tolerant pattern of political behavior than is found in the rest of the nation.

Although there are some differences between the core culture and these mainly white religious groups, these variances are rather minor compared to

*Generally, people who are better educated and wealthier are more likely to support civil liberties but are opposed to increased expansion of the welfare state.

The Ethnic Factor

the blacks. Black Americans are more than an ethnic group; they are to a large extent a subculture quite distinct from the rest of the society. Whereas, in the studies of other groups, we only had data on adult political behavior (usually voting) from which to speculate, with blacks there are some studies of the actual political socialization process. These studies reveal, as one might imagine, an important divergence from the dominant political themes of the core culture.

It is necessary, however, to examine what those dominant themes are first and then to compare them to the responses of both black and poor white children. Such an examination will take us beyond the personal world of the child and its immediate social nexus into the life of the community where the political socialization process becomes more formal and tempered by political realities.

Summary

The patterns of differentiation begin to exhibit themselves very early in the life of an individual. We know from considerable evidence that both the effects of sex and class differences do have an impact on the child's political socialization. Interest and participation in politics is more accentuated among males than females. Citizens from the more affluent strata of our society are more likely to be politically active than those who are less well off.

We can see also that peer groups are more concerned with transmitting cultural tastes than they are with forming the young citizen's political views. However, for a significant minority, peer groups are an important influence in explaining their changing views and increased mobilization. Still the best evidence of peer group influence is adult reference groups which often give political cues to their members and socialize them into occupational roles.

Lastly, it is also obvious that there is no single melting pot socialization process. Ethnic differences remain. It is less apparent how national background influences a child's thinking, but there is considerable evidence that some children from different religions and races are experiencing quite varying patterns of socialization.

Notes

1. For evidence of the comparative aggressiveness of males, see Albert Bandura, D. Ross, and S. A. Ross, "Transmission of Aggression through Imitation of Aggressive Models," *Journal of Abnormal and Social Psychology*, 63 (1961), 575–582; J. Kagan

and J. Lemkin, "The Child's Differential Perception of Parental Attributes," *Journal of Abnormal and Social Psychology*, 61 (1960), 440–447; E. M. Bennett and L. R. Cohen, "Men and Women: Personality Patterns and Contrasts," *Genetic Psychology Monographs*, 60 (1959), 101–153; and J. Kagan, B. Hosken, and S. Watson, "The Child's Symbolic Conceptualization of the Parents," *Child Development*, 32 (1961), 625–636. Other studies show that women in all age groups are more dependent, conformist, and socially passive: R. S. Crutchfield, "Conformity and Character," *American Psychologist*, 10 (1955), 191–198; J. Kagan and H. A. Moss, *Birth to Maturity* (New York: Wiley, 1962); and C. I. Hovland and I. L. Janis, eds., *Personality and Persuasibility* (New Haven, Conn.: Yale University Press, 1959).

2. There are examples of the varied types of "appropriate" sex roles in Margaret Mead, *Sex and Temperament in Three Primitive Societies* (New York: Morrow, 1935) although most of the literature shows a great deal of cross-cultural regularities as in R. D'Andrde, "Cross Cultural Studies of Sex Differences in Behavior," *The Development of Sex Differences*, edited by Eleanor Maccoby, (Stanford, Calif.: Stanford University Press, 1966).

3. Cited in Fred I. Greenstein, *Children and Politics* (New Haven, Conn.: Yale University Press, 1965), p. 126. For a longer discussion of female political participation, see Harriet Holter, *Sex Role and Social Structure* (Oslo: Universitetsforlaget, 1970), chap. 5. David Easton and Jack Dennis, *Children in the Political System* (New York: McGraw-Hill, 1969) finds that the level of differences is much lower than studies have indicated.

4. Angus Campbell, et. al., *The American Voter* (New York: Wiley, 1960), p. 487. Kagan and Moss, *Birth to Maturity*, finds that there is some evidence that the higher the educational level the more likely a woman will choose to be involved in so-called masculine activities. Also, girls tested in 1960 were found to be more "masculine" in their game choices than those tested in 1930. See B. G. Rosenberg and B. Sutton-Smith, "A Revised Conception of Masculine-Feminine Differences in Play Activities," *Journal of Genetic Psychology*, 96 (1960), 165–170. Sex typing is still strong in the lower class as can be seen in M. L. Kohn, "Social Class and Parental Values," *American Journal of Sociology*, 64 (1959), 337–351.

5. Campbell, et. al., *The American Voter*, p. 490.

6. Campbell, p. 491.

7. Greenstein, *Children and Politics*, pp. 107–110; James G. March, "Husband-Wife Interaction over Political Issues," *Public Opinion Quarterly*, 17 (Winter 1953), 461–470.

8. Greenstein, *Children and Politics*, pp. 115–117.

9. S. M. Lipset, *Political Man* (New York: Anchor Books, 1960), chap. 5 and Frank Pinner, "Parental Overprotection and Political Disorder," *The Annals*, 361 (September 1965), 58–70. Urie Bronfenbrenner, "Socialization and Social Class through Time and Space," *Readings in Social Psychology*, edited by Eleanor Maccoby, et. al., pp. 400–424 maintains that many of the differences may be explained by the greater receptivity of the middle class to the popularized advice of specialists on infant care.

10. Robert Lane, *Political Life* (New York: Free Press, 1959), pp. 233–234.

11. Greenstein, *Children and Politics*, p. 96 finds that there was no significant difference in the tendency of children, regardless of class, to have a party identification.

12. Greenstein, pp. 95–106. Also of interest is Robert Hess and Judith V. Torney, *The Development of Political Attitudes in Children* (New York: Anchor Books, 1967).

13. Peer groups are discussed succinctly in John E. Horrocks, *The Psychology of Adolescence* (Boston: Houghton Mifflin, 1969) and in Ernest W. Campbell, "Adolescent Socialization," *Handbook of Socialization Theory and Research*, edited by David Golsin (Chicago: Rand McNally, 1969), pp. 821–861.

14. H. H. Remmers and D. H. Radler, *The American Teenager* (Indianapolis: Bobbs-Merrill, 1957).

15. James Samuel Coleman, *The Adolescent Society* (New York: Free Press, 1961). An older study which is still useful is August Hollingshead, *Elmstown's Youth* (New York: Wiley, 1949).

16. Urie Bronfenbrenner, *Two Worlds of Childhood: U.S. and U.S.S.R.* (New York: Russell Sage Foundation, 1970).

17. D. Matza, "Subterranean Traditions of Youth," *The Annals*, 338 (November 1961), 102–118 argues that the youth culture really plays at social deviancy and avoids the real thing. A comprehensive view of the generational conflict is presented in Samuel N. Eisenstadt, *From Generation to Generation* (Glencoe: Free Press, 1956).

18. Elizabeth Douvan and Joseph Adelson, *The Adolescent Experience* (New York: Wiley, 1966), p. 81.

19. Douvan and Adelson, p. 84. Also see Kenneth Keniston, *Young Radicals* (New York: Harcourt, Brace & World, 1968).

20. Peter Rose, "Student Opinion on the 1956 Presidential Election," *Public Opinion Quarterly*, 21 (Fall 1957), 371–376 and Theodore M. Newcomb, *Personality and Social Change* (New York: Dryden Press, 1943).

21. Remmers and Radler, *The American Teenager;* D. C. Epperson, "A Reassessment of Indices of Parental Influence in 'The Adolescent Society'," *American Sociological Review*, 29 (1964), 93–96; B. C. Rosen, "The Reference Group Approach to the Parental Factor in Attitude and Behavior Formation," *Social Forces*, 34 (1955), 137–144; R. Middleton and S. Putney, "Political Expression of Adolescent Rebellion," *American Journal of Sociology*, 68 (1963), 527–535; and R. A. Dentler and L. J. Monroe, "The Family and Early Adolescent Conformity and Deviance," *Marriage and Family Living*, 23 (1961), 241–247. Douvan and Adelson, *The Adolescent Experience*, chap. 5, indicates that among girls the percentage of those who think parental rules are fair and right increases from ages twelve to fourteen to ages seventeen to eighteen.

22. Kenneth Langton, *Political Socialization* (New York: Oxford University Press, 1969), pp. 125, 131.

23. Langton, pp. 158–160 finds that among the working and middle class, the politicized family accounted for more highly efficacious offspring than did the peer group or school. However, among the upper class, the peer group is more dominant in instilling a high sense of efficacy.

24. Campbell, et. al, *The American Voter*, chap. 12. The term *peer group* is rather broad in its usage and I have used it to refer to a variety of nonfamilial reference groups. For a detailed discussion see Muzafer Sherif and Carolyn W. Sherif, *Reference Groups* (New York: Harper & Row, 1964).

25. There are many studies in this area; two good collections are Robert Peabody and Nelson Polsby, eds., *New Perspectives on the House of Representatives* (Chicago: Rand McNally, 1969) and Raymond E. Wolfinger, ed., *Readings on Congress* (Englewood Cliffs, N. J.: Prentice-Hall, 1971).

26. Two surveys of ethnic groups are Nathan Glazer and Daniel P. Moynihan, *Beyond the Melting Pot* (Cambridge, Mass.: MIT Press, 1966) and Milton Gordon, *Assimilation in American Life* (New York: Oxford University Press, 1964). Political scientists have begun to take an interest in ethnic groups aside from voting. See Edgar

Litt, *Beyond Pluralism* (Glenview, Ill.: Scott, Foresman, 1970); and the anthologies of Harry Bailey, Jr. and Ellis Katz, eds., *Ethnic Group Politics* (Columbus, Ohio: Charles E. Merrill Books, Inc., 1969); and Lawrence H. Fuchs, ed., *American Ethnic Politics* (New York: Harper & Row, 1968).

27. Charles H. Anderson, *White Protestant Americans* (Englewood Cliffs, N. J. Prentice-Hall, 1970), passim.

28. Besides the above studies, some other related works are: Herbert Gans, *The Urban Villagers*, (New York: Free Press, 1962); Giles Edward Gobetz, "The Ethnic Ethics of Assimilation: Slovenian View," *Phylon*, 27 (Fall 1966), 268–273; Francis A. J. Ianni, "The Italo-American Teenager," *The Annals*, 338 (November 1961), 70–78; and Theodore Saloutos, *The Greek in the United States* (Cambridge, Mass.: Harvard University Press, 1964).

29. This view is examined in Milton Gordon, *Assimilation in American Life*, and in Will Herberg, *Protestant-Catholic-Jew* (Garden City, N. Y.: Doubleday, 1955).

30. Gerhard Lenski, *The Religious Factor* (New York: Anchor Books, 1963), chap. 4.

31. Lenski also finds that white Protestants are more tolerant, followed by Jews, Catholics, and blacks.

32. Andrew Greeley and Peter Rossi, *The Education of Catholic Americans* (Chicago: Aldine, 1966).

33. Lawrence H. Fuchs, *The Political Behavior of American Jews* (Glencoe, Ill.: Free Press, 1956). The basis for the observation on civic mindedness comes from the much discussed article by James Q. Wilson and Edward C. Banfield, "Public Regardingness as a Value Premise in Voting Behavior," *American Political Science Review*, 58 (December 1964), 876–887, which argues that white Protestants and Jews are more likely to support public expenditures even if they do not benefit from them. Other white ethnic groups, as the Poles, Czechs, Irish, and Italians are much more reluctant to do so unless it is in their own interest.

five

The Child's Political Community

The first three stages which we have examined represent important phases in the development of the child. Some characteristics of these stages, such as the propensity for imitation, a person retains for the rest of his life. Other characteristics, such as the levels of trust and self-esteem, are a part of his primary learning experiences and are subject to reinforcement or contradiction throughout life.

The focal points of these latent stages are really only the family and a few playmates. A major step forward occurs when the child begins to move into the larger community and realizes that he is a part of an abstract association. It is at this stage of Communitarianism that the child acquires a manifest political sensibility—one which allows him to identify with people he has not seen or may never see. Adults tend to take this development for granted, but when one stops to consider, it is rather remarkable how the young child comes to conceptualize notions of community, government, and authority.

The Benevolent State

It is difficult to state at what exact age children first become aware of political authority. It is probably before the age of seven because recent studies show that even in grade two almost three-quarters of the students thought they knew what the word government meant (although probably some really did not). Yet even at this early age, children begin to realize the importance of authority figures and are likely to point to the President and the policeman as primary examples.[1]

As might be expected, the young child first focuses his attention on the personal aspects of political authority. When asked what the government is, the child will often point to particular individuals or historical figures rather than to political institutions or legal procedures. But as he matures, the child begins to deemphasize personalities and becomes more aware of what words like democracy, law, and nation mean. His political perspective grows larger and more sophisticated so that by the fifth grade, the child is more likely to answer that Congress, and not the President, is the primary law-giving authority in America. Thus in a few short years, the child's focus has moved from personalization to symbolic formulations to rational, legal structures.[2]

In addition, the child's conceptualization of government also changes. At first, he takes a collectivist attitude toward government and approves of its paternalism and intervention. When asked to name the main characteristics of government, the child usually emphasizes that it is important, knowledgeable, helpful, nearly infallible, and able to reward and punish people. There are some changes in these attitudes as the child grows older. As Figure 5.1 shows, from grades four to eight the power, knowledge, and leadership aspects of the government are emphasized while the infallible and helpful characteristics become less important.[3] Still, even among older children, the government retains a remarkably high rating.

One of the central figures in the child's political world is, of course, the President. Easton and Dennis maintain that they were unable to find one child in their predominantly white sample of 12,000 children who did not express the highest esteem for the Chief Executive. For younger children, he was the ideal adult: benevolent, dependable, trustworthy, and infallible. Above all, they were aware of his great powers and they approved of his leadership. Of course, there is some decline in the President's standing as one moves up the different grade levels—but he is still viewed in a very approving way even by older children.[4] (See Figure 5.2.)

However, it is important to realize that even young children are able to associate the President with certain issues. He is not just a larger than life father figure, but rather the President is seen as being involved in public controversies and political decisions. In fact, children are more likely to add to a President's favorable rating if he has the same partisan affiliation as they (and their parents) have.[5]

A second figure of importance to the child is the policeman. One would think that this position is simply due to the fact that he is the local embodiment of authority. However, very young children, at least, do not realize that government can be local. To them all government is fused into one large mass, unmarked by adult differentiations. Gradually though, children come to real-

Figure 5.1
Mean Ratings by Grade on Five Attributes of Government

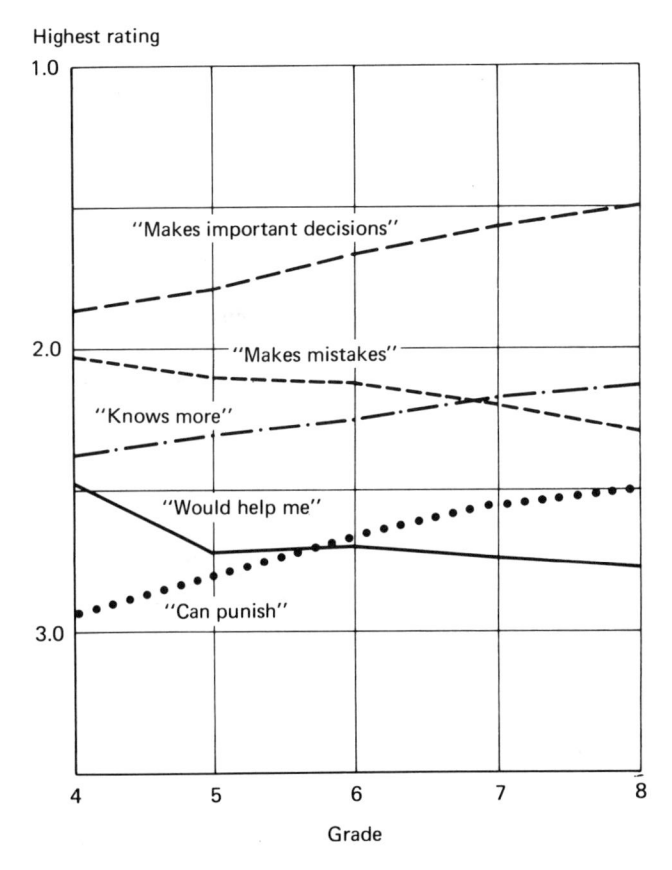

[Figure: Line graph with y-axis "Highest rating" from 1.0 to 3.0 and x-axis "Grade" from 4 to 8, showing five lines labeled "Makes important decisions", "Makes mistakes", "Knows more", "Would help me", and "Can punish".]

Source: From *Children in the Political System* by David Easton and Jack Dennis, p. 135. Copyright 1969 by McGraw-Hill. Used with permission of McGraw-Hill Book Company.

ize that the policeman is not the maker of the law but rather its enforcer. By the age of eight or nine, the policeman is seen as the guardian of the rules which are arrived at through community consensus (Stage III).

Easton and Dennis maintain that this childhood orientation toward the policeman is crucial for the maintainence of the system. If citizens, when they are still quite young, come to distrust one of the major authority figures then the whole system would suffer. This would mean that the President would

Figure 5.2

Mean Ratings by Grade on Thirteen Attributes of the President

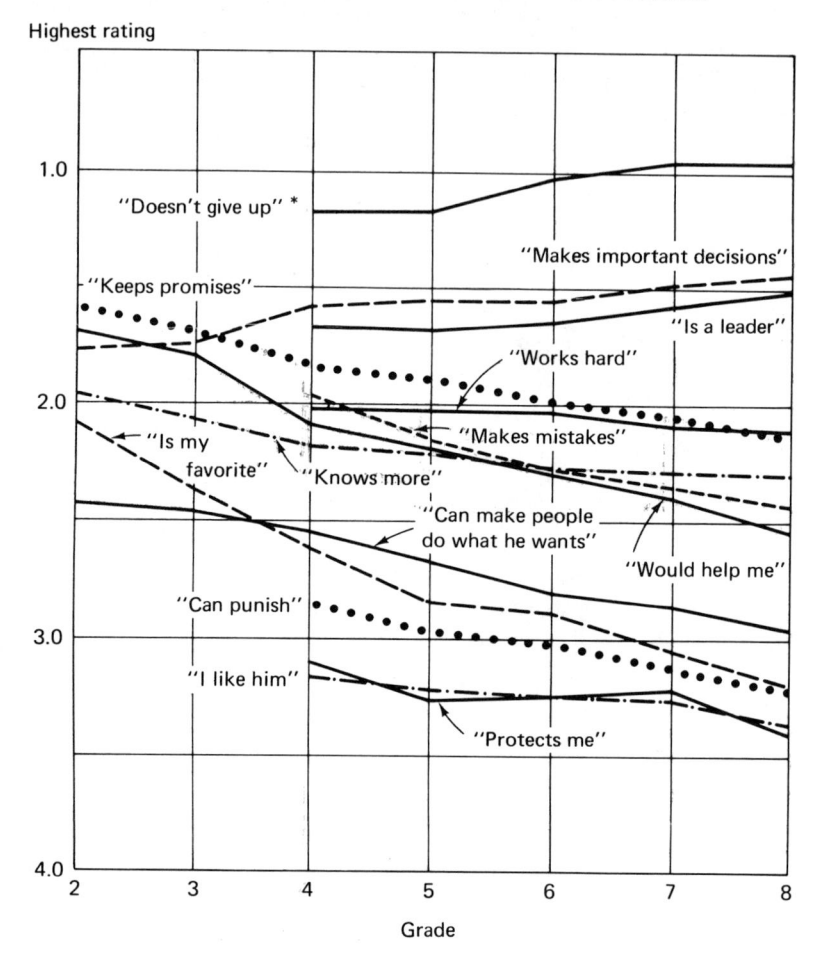

*Means of this rating were subtracted from 6.0 to make them comparable to the rest.
Source: From *Children in the Political System* by David Easton and Jack Dennis, p. 178. Copyright 1969 by McGraw-Hill. Used with permission of McGraw-Hill Book Company.

have to bear the full burden for generating diffuse support for the system among younger children.[6]

As children grow older, they develop also some sort of allegiance to specific political institutions. From grades four to eight, children begin to think less in terms of personalization than in terms of political institutions. For example, children come to realize what the specific roles of Congress and the Supreme Court are in the system. One of the most interesting aspects of this development is that while children become more sophisticated and critical at each successive level, they still retain a deep respect for the Supreme Court. The Court is seen as making fewer mistakes than the President, the Government, the Senator, the policeman, and the father. Children in grade four and those in grade eight feel approximately the same on the question of the Court's relative infallibility.[7]

The Young Citizen

Most of the major political socialization studies agree on one point: the child has a strong orientation toward political compliance. In their survey, Hess and Torney have found that such compliance is due to four main causes: a positive feeling toward government (especially the Presidency); a considerable respect for authority figures in general; a child's experience in subordinate, compliant roles; and a normative belief that all systems of rules are fair.[8]

Undoubtedly, children are also quite impressed with power and often tend to associate it with benevolence when they judge authority figures. In addition, they also seem to trust the good intentions of the government and its basic fairness. For them, laws and rules are really the same thing; in each case, organized social activity requires regulation and such regulation is welcomed by children. Younger children, especially, tend to see laws as being ancient, unchanging, and just (as in Stage II, Command Morality). But as they grow older, children begin to reexamine what the functions of law really are. They come to place more emphasis on the law's role in helping to run the country than on punishing people.[9] Table 5.1 shows this development from grades two to eight.

In school, the child becomes increasingly concerned with the importance of civic virtues. In the early grades, the good citizen is seen by children as being synonymous with the good person; he is helpful, polite, clean, careful, and hardworking. As children grow older, they see citizenship in more political terms—voting, participation, and public concern.[10]

Also, children begin to reexamine their definition of democracy and public participation much more. At first, children have some vague notion that democracy involves "rule by the people," but they are not too sure how this rule operates. However, as Table 5.2 shows, children gradually come to identify democracy with popular rule, voting, and a general notion of equality.[11]

It is therefore not surprising that older children believe that voting is one of the most important symbols of the American political system. While

Table 5.1

Changes by Grade in Perception of Function of Laws

Grade level	Number of cases	To punish people	To run country	To keep people from doing bad things	To keep people safe
2	198	16.2%	6.6%	16.7%	60.6%
3	217	7.4	14.3	14.7	63.6
4	211	6.6	14.7	13.3	65.4
5	210	3.3	20.0	10.5	66.2
6	233	3.9	27.0	14.6	54.5
7	226	4.0	28.3	8.0	59.7
8	89	2.2	34.8	9.0	53.9

Notes   Item: Why do we have laws? Put an X beside the one that is most true. (From Pilot Study 14 questionnaire.)
Significance Unit: 10%

Source: Reprinted from Robert D. Hess and Judith V. Torney, *The Development of Political Attitudes in Children* (New York: Anchor Books, 1967), p. 60; copyright © by Robert D. Hess and Judith V. Torney 1967. Reprinted by permission of the authors and Aldine · Atherton, Inc.

only 4 percent of the second graders mentioned voting when asked to choose "the best picture of government," over 46 percent of the eighth graders chose it. In addition, there is a sharp increase in the number of positive responses after grade four and five on the topic of political efficacy and by age nine or ten, children are more likely to be engaging in political discussions with family and friends.[12]

Generally, what is most striking about the attitudes of American children and even adults is the considerable pride they take in the political system. There have been many studies which have asked citizens of various nations what aspect of their country gave them the greatest feelings of pride. While citizens of other countries tend to stress their economic system, the beauty of their land, or their religious solidarity, the overwhelming majority of the American respondents cite representative institutions, the Constitution, and political liberty. Undoubtedly, such strong feelings of political allegiance are inculcated at a very early age in children.[13]

Abstract Allegiance

With this strong interest in the community, children come to emphasize the consensual aspects of politics and to play down conflict. This may be due to the formal instruction of the school, which strongly stresses political agree-

Table 5.2
Changes by Grade in Concept of Democracy (Percentages Answering "Yes" for Each Definition)

Grade level	The people rule	No one is rich or poor	All grown-ups can vote	All have equal chance	You can say things against the government	If most agree, the rest should go along
4	26.0%	19.4%	39.4%	35.8%	15.4%	29.9%
5	35.9	24.3	52.4	50.2	23.0	35.5
6	51.9	27.1	69.0	66.4	39.1	35.2
7	64.3	24.2	75.4	76.8	48.6	28.2
8	76.4	22.7	75.3	82.8	53.5	27.6
Teachers	98.4	7.5	76.5	88.3	55.0	67.6

Notes Items: What is a democracy? [In each of the following questions, choose one: (1) Yes; (2) No; (3) Don't know.] (37) Is a democracy where people rule? (38) Is a democracy where no one is very rich or very poor? (39) Is a democracy where all grown-ups can vote? (40) Is a democracy where everyone has an equal chance to get ahead? (41) Is a democracy where you can say anything against the government without getting into trouble? (42) Is a democracy where if most of the people agree, the rest should go along?
  N ranged from 1530 to 1787 for students and from 373 to 375 for teachers.
  Significance Units: 3% for all items.

Source: Reprinted from Robert D. Hess and Judith V. Torney, *The Development of Political Attitudes in Children* (New York: Anchor Books, 1967), p. 75; copyright © by Robert D. Hess and Judith V. Torney 1967. Reprinted by permission of the authors and Aldine · Atherton, Inc.

ment and harmony; or it may be due to the child's own feeling that conflict and divisiveness are dangerous. In any case, children become more aware of the existence of the nation-state and more concerned over its unity. For example, children feel that the defeated candidates should help the winners, and this feeling *increases* with each successive grade level. Many children, especially the younger ones, do not see campaigns as being devisive at all; in the rather lively 1960 Presidential race, 70 percent of the third graders in one sample thought that neither of the candidates had said anything bad about the other. Thus children seem to stress the consensual aspects of elections and lay great importance on the general rules of morality which they think should surround such activities.[14]

When they are quite young, children regard partisan conflict as being highly undesirable, and they cannot understand what the real differences are between the political parties. But as they grow older, they begin to take more interest in participating and are quite likely to have a partisan affiliation. From grades two to eight, the percentage of children with an affiliation jumps from

Abstract Allegiance

45 percent to 85 percent. Even though it is obvious that children by and large inherit their party preference, the children themselves say that each person should make up his mind about politics and not necessarily follow his parents.[15]

Gradually, the child's early orientation toward the community takes on a more forceful and political tone. From grade four or five and continuing to grade eight, the child begins to develop a conscious awareness of the existence of his nation and its role vis-à-vis others. This fifth stage, which entails a sense of patriotic nationalism, can best be termed Abstract Allegiance. At this stage, children become more concerned with the uniqueness and unity of their nation. They feel pride in its real or supposed accomplishments and recognize that being American, French, or Swiss implies something quite different. They are also quite willing to state that while they do not want to change their nationality, they can also see why other children from foreign lands would not want to change theirs.[16] Thus the nation becomes a specific and quite concrete reality that has a right to ask for each citizen's respect and allegiance.

Places Elsewhere

From the discussion above, one can see that the major socialization studies have described a rather placid vision. American children are being effectively inculcated into political attitudes that are supportive of the system and they, in turn, hold strong feelings of benevolence and trust in the government. From their earliest years through secondary school, children seem to exhibit quite positive cognitive and affective inclinations toward authority figures. It seems, then, that like the popularized view of our history, the political socialization process is a continuing success story.

Yet the events of the last decade do not seem to lend much credence to this placid formulation. As political scientists continued to analyze other samples, they found that some subcultures of poverty, both black and white, did not share the predominant patterns of socialization. The image of authority and the attitudes toward government which children from these areas have are quite different from the white, middle-class samples that gave us the evidence for the generalizations made above.

In this regard, one interesting study was done by Dean Jaros and his associates in the rural Appalachian area of Knox County, Kentucky with children from grades five to twelve. When asked to evaluate the President, these children had significantly less favorable impressions than did the children from the previous studies. Compared with most men, the President did not fare too well; in fact, about a quarter of the youngsters expressed overtly unfavorable reactions to him. Among high school seniors, only 31 percent thought that the President liked almost everybody while an equal percentage thought that he liked fewer people than most men. The study also showed that not one twelfth grader thought that the President was the best person in the world and, more importantly, near one-third felt that he was not a good person at all. Interestingly, there is little change in the attitudes of children in this sample from one grade level to another. The picture presented is of a rather static sense of disillusionment and distrust.

The single most striking finding in the Knox study is the very high level of political cynicism among children. The entire fifth to twelfth grade group is significantly more cynical than the twelfth graders alone in other major studies. Table 5.3 compares the level of cynicism of the Knox County sample with the Survey Research Center's nationwide sample of high school seniors.

This Knox County study has been expanded by one of the coauthors,

Table 5.3
Political Cynicism Scores*

		Knox County data (whole sample)	Knox County data (high school only)	SRC national sample	Smirnov two-sample test
Most cynical	6	8%	26%	5%	Knox County data (whole sample) and SRC national sample,
	5	11	22	3	$D = .16, p < .001$
	4	19	11	13	
	3	19	20	37	Knox County data (high school only) and SRC national sample
	2	23	15	25	$D = .40, p < .001$
Least cynical	1	21	6	17	
		101%	100%	100%	
Number of cases		305	54	1869	

*It has been assumed that the Political Cynicism Scale generated Guttman scalar patterns in the Knox County data as it did in the SRC national sample. To compensate for the possible invalidity of this assumption, the items were conservatively dichotomized and conservatively scored. Only choice of the most cynical available alternative was considered a cynical response. Failure of a respondent to choose the most cynical alternative for whatever reason, including nonresponse, resulted in the recording of a noncynical item score.

Source: Dean Jaros, Herbert Hirsch, and Frederic J. Fleron, Jr., "The Malevolent Leader: Political Socialization in an American Sub-culture," *American Political Science Review*, 62 (June 1968), p. 570.

Herbert Hirsch, in order to find out which agents of socialization are most important. Hirsch discovered that, as in the study of middle-class children, there is a strong association between parents and their offspring on the question of partisan identification. In Knox County also it is the mother, with her strong influence in this white subculture of poverty, who is the main reason for this partisan tie.

However, there is one complication; while the mother may be more effective in transmitting her partisan allegiance, it is the father who is more influential in giving voting cues to his offspring. This influence is not related to whether he is employed or not, but it does increase at each educational level. Overall, there is a tendency for these children to listen to their parents (especially their father) longer for voting advice than children in other studies, thus indicating an increased political dependence.

On the question of peer groups, there is again little evidence that they are effective in transmitting or challenging political values in this subculture. Peer groups do not replace the parents as sources of information even as the children grow older. Nor do these groups disturb the family's influence on questions of partisanship and voting. The only importance that the peer group has is that it does transmit some information on local government, but very little on state or national government.

Except for the media, the most important agent for transmitting political information is the school. Formal instruction in civics apparently does have more of a result among the lower class than among the other classes. For the white students of Appalachia (and as we will see, for black ghetto students), those who have had a civics course do indicate that they have profited from it in some way. The Knox County students who had these courses were more likely to seek out the news, express an interest in politics, and have a higher level of knowledge than those who did not take such courses. In addition, the role of the school as a salient source of political advice also increases from one successive grade to another.

Of all the findings in Hirsch's study, however, the most interesting one deals with the mass media. He found that radio was the most important source of information on state and local issues, while television performed the same function for national and international questions. There was no variation from one grade level to another, a fact which indicates that the role of the media is remarkably pervasive even for young children.

Yet the real importance of the media lies in its latent rather than in its manifest aspect. While there is no relationship between the content of what is watched or read and political knowledge, there is a relationship between the rate of exposure and political knowledge. Thus it is not the content but the quantity which is of crucial concern. There is one interesting complication: where such an increase in knowledge does occur, it is mainly due not to the electronic media but to the newspapers. Those people who are more politically aware are those who read newspapers more often.[18] Unfortunately, social scientists know very little about the role of television and radio in our political life.

The Knox Country study is important because it presents a different portrait of the political socialization process. If this rural white subculture shows some striking differences from the previous studies, it is because the America that these children live in and relate to is quite different from the America of middle-class youngsters. Obviously, if this is the case with Appalachian children, it is even more true for black children.

In the last decade or so, a major alteration in the political consciousness of black Americans has occurred and has spilled over to other ethnic groups as well. Many previous studies of black political behavior have emphasized their apathy and lack of interest in consensual politics. However, these studies did not distinguish between indifference and a submerged, but pervasive feeling of hostility toward white America and its institutions.[19]

In part, it is difficult to fathom the depths of these feelings because many black citizens are becoming reluctant to be a part of social science research. Some of their leaders have argued, with obvious justification, that it is white America that must be analyzed and altered. Fortunately for our purposes, there are a few studies on the political socialization of black children from which we can make some general statements about early attitudes and beliefs.

One such study was done by Edward Greenberg in schools in Philadelphia and Pittsburgh. He found that children of both races have substantially similar responses on questions of community support, such as national pride and love of the flag. However, blacks are still a little less supportive and by grade nine, there was some difference between black and white responses.

More marked differences occurred when children had to judge how helpful, concerned, and trustful the government was. Both black and white students have a high regard in the early grades, but by grade nine there is somewhat of a drop in their level of esteem. As Figure 5.3 shows, this drop occurs earlier and is more pronounced with black children than with white ones.

A different response pattern occurs when one analyzes the attitudes of black children toward authority figures such as the President and the policeman. While the idealization of the President drops at each grade level, this drop again occurs more rapidly in the case of black students. Yet by grade nine, there is a reversal of this decline. Apparently, by then black children begin to become aware of Federal activity in the area of civil rights and credit it to the Chief Executive. With regard to the policeman, he is held in high esteem by children of both races. Yet his position too begins to decline—precipitously in the case of black youngsters. As might be expected, the policeman is liked least by lower-class, black males.[20]

Figure 5.3

Index of Government Support: Percent of Children Scoring 3 on the Index

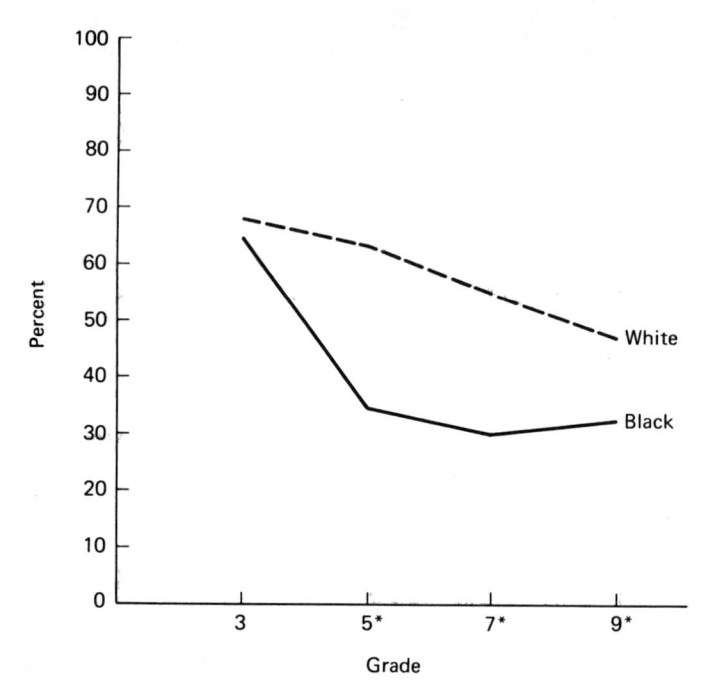

*Differences between black and white children significant at .05 level.

Note: A score of 3 indicates that children had the highest support for the government.

Source: Edward Greenberg, "Black Children and the Political System," *Public Opinion Quarterly*, 34 (Fall 1970), p. 339.

In addition, those black children who have a more accurate perception of race relations tend to exhibit the greatest erosion of support for the government. However, blacks do acknowledge the greater efforts of the Federal government on their behalf. For example, at first black children say they have the most confidence in the local government, followed by the state government, and then the Federal government. By grade nine, this order is reversed. It seems that one of the major supports of the system and one which has apparently prevented even deeper black disenchantment has been the concern of the Federal government for civil rights during the period in which these studies were done.[21]

The final question to be examined is that of political participation and efficacy. Not surprisingly, black children are more subject than participant oriented in their views toward politics. While they do recognize the Federal government as being a benevolent and protective force, they still feel that the total political system is not responsive to the demands of the people.[23] Generally, black children do not believe that their efforts have much of an effect on governmental decisions or public policy.

These findings have been underscored by a study of black children in Toledo, Ohio that was done by Schley Lyons. It was found that blacks, regardless of where they lived in the city, had a lower sense of efficacy and a greater degree of cynicism than did white students. High school blacks felt less efficacious than junior high school whites; elementary school blacks were about as cynical toward politics as were senior high school whites. Thus being black is a much stronger predictor of a low sense of efficacy and a high level of cynicism than is milieu, sex, or even grade level. Lyons also found that students, both black and white, who live in the slums and do well in school are more likely to feel efficacious. Thus, as in the Knox County study, it appears that the school does have some important effects on the political socialization process.*

Summary

As far as the child's early orientations toward the political community are concerned, it is necessary to examine both the community and the subculture in which he lives. Students from middle-class backgrounds regard the government as benevolent and trustworthy and they relate positively to symbols of authority, especially the President and the policeman. At Stage IV of development, the child acquires strong communal ties to the polity, ties that he accepts more than he examines. But as time goes on, he comes to depersonalize the political world and develop attachments in a very deep way to his nation-state and its place in the world.

For those who do not share in these feelings of benevolence and trust, their reaction is one of cynicism toward authority and the government. They come to feel alienated from politics and are less likely to develop a strong sense of Abstract Allegiance. Their cynicism, combined with feelings of inefficacy and distrust, dissuades them from thinking that politics can be a meaningful and rewarding personal concern.

*As the next chapter will show, the later years of schooling are probably a more crucial period for disadvantaged children than they are for middle-class children.

Notes

1. David Easton and Jack Dennis, *Children in the Political System* (New York: McGraw-Hill, 1969), p. 113. This study of 12,000 school children from ages seven to fourteen was done in all four areas of the country for the period 1961–1962. Nearly all members of the sample were white.

2. Easton and Dennis, p. 117. The Easton and Dennis formulation follows fairly closely that of Fred I. Greenstein, *Children and Politics* (New Haven, Conn.: Yale University Press, 1965).

3. Easton and Dennis, *Children in the Political System*, p. 135.

4. Easton and Dennis, pp. 177–178. A more critical view is found in Dean Jaros, "Children's Orientations toward the President," *Journal of Politics*, 29 (May 1967), 368–387.

5. Easton and Dennis, *Children in the Political System*, p. 195; Roberta Sigel, "An Exploration into Some Aspects of Political Socialization: School Children's Reaction to the Death of a President," *Children and the Death of a President*, edited by Martha Wolfenstein and Gilbert Kliman (New York: Doubleday, 1965), pp. 30-61, which shows that Democratic children were more severely affected by Kennedy's assassination than were Republican children. Also of interest are her "Image of the American Presidency: Part II of an Exploration into Popular Views of Presidential Power," *Midwest Journal of Political Science*, 10 (February 1966), 123–137 and "Image of a President: Some Insights into the Political Views of School Children," *American Political Science Review*, 62 (March 1968), 216–226.

6. Easton and Dennis, *Children in the Political System*, p. 240. For a discussion of how children are differentially socialized to each level of government, see M. Kent Jennings, "Pre-Adult Orientations to Multiple Systems of Government," *Midwest Journal of Political Science*, 11 (August 1967), 291–317.

7. Easton and Dennis, *Children in the Political System*, pp. 263, 252. Adults are apparently more critical of the courts according to Kenneth M. Dolbeare, "The Public Views the Supreme Court," *Law, Politics, and the Federal Courts*, edited by Herbert Jacobs (Boston: Little, Brown, 1967), pp. 194–212.

8. Robert Hess and Judith V. Torney, *The Development of Political Attitudes in Children* (New York: Anchor Books, 1967), p. 68. This is a study of 17,000 children (mostly white) begun in 1960. Hess and Easton had originally worked together on a series of pilot studies on political socialization which are cited in the Hess and Torney bibliography.

9. Hess and Torney, p. 60.

10. Hess and Torney, p. 45.

11. Hess and Torney, p. 75.

12. Hess and Torney, pp. 41, 81.

13. Gabriel Almond and Sidney Verba, *The Civic Culture* (Princeton: Princeton University Press, 1963), pp. 102–103; Reid Reading, "Political Socialization in Columbia and the United States," *Midwest Journal of Political Science*, 12 (August 1968), 352–381; and A. B. Hodgetts, *What Culture? What Heritage? A Study of Civic Education in Canada* (Ontario: Ontario Institute for Studies in Education, 1968). Also relevant is the entire issue of *Comparative Political Studies* 3 (July 1970).

14. Hess and Torney, *The Development of Political Attitudes*, pp. 89–90.

15. Hess and Torney, p. 96.

16. Jean Piaget and Anne-Marie Weil, "The Development in Children of the

Idea of the Homeland and Relations with Other Countries," *International Social Science Bulletin*, 3 (1951), 561–578; Gustav Jahoda, "The Development of Children's Ideas about Country and Nationality, Part I: The Conceptual Framework," *British Journal of Educational Psychology*, 33 (1963), 47–60 and his "The Development of Children's Ideas about Country and Nationality, Part II: National Symbols and Themes, *British Journal of Educational Psychology*, 33 (1963), 143–153.

17. Dean Jaros, Herbert Hirsch, and Frederic J. Fleron, "The Malevolent Leader: Political Socialization in an American Sub-culture," *American Political Science Review*, 62 (June 1968), 564–575. Political scientists have generally ignored the question of whether the particular incumbent in the Presidency may affect the feelings that children have at that time.

18. Herbert Hirsch, *Poverty and Politicization* (New York: Free Press, 1971), passim.

19. William Brink and Louis Harris, *Black and White* (New York: Simon and Schuster, 1966) and John S. Jackson, "The Political Behavior and Socio-Economic Background of Black Students: The Antecedents of Protest," *Midwest Journal of Political Science*, 15 (November 1971), 661–686.

20. Edward S. Greenberg, "Black Children and the Political System," *Public Opinion Quarterly*, 34 (Fall 1970), 337–338. See also Dwaine Marvick, "The Political Socialization of the American Negro," *The Annals*, 361 (September 1965), 112–137 and William C. Kvaraceus, et. al., *Negro Self Concept: Implications for School and Citizenship* (New York: McGraw-Hill, 1965).

21. Edward S. Greenberg, "Children and Government: A Comparison Across Racial Lines," *Midwest Journal of Political Science*, 14 (May 1970), 265; Greenberg, "Children and the Political Community: A Comparison Across Racial Lines," *Canadian Journal of Political Science*, 2 (December 1969), 471–492; and Harrell R. Rodgers and George Taylor, "The Policeman as an Agent of Regime Legitimation," *Midwest Journal of Political Science*, 15 (February 1971), 84. Of course if the Federal government's attitude toward civil rights changes, the corollary argument is that one of the major sources of support for the system would be eliminated.

22. Rodgers and Taylor, "The Policeman as an Agent of Regime Legitimation," 80, 81, 86.

23. Greenberg, "Children and Politics," 273.

24. Schley R. Lyons, "The Political Socialization of Ghetto Children: Efficacy and Cynicism," *Journal of Politics*, 32 (May 1970), 297–305. See also William H. Form and Joan Huber, "Income, Race, and the Ideology of Political Efficacy," *Journal of Politics*, 33 (August 1971), 659–688.

six

The Role of the School

The major formal institution of American political socialization is the public school. Indeed, one of the principle purposes of the school system has been and still is to provide a common standard of citizenship into which all Americans are to be educated. From Horace Mann to John Dewey, educators have stressed civic inculcation as one important way of overcoming cultural pluralism.[1] This historical concern explains why schoolmen, despite their well-known record for lethargy, have continually reexamined the goals of citizenship education, especially in this century.

One scholar, Daniel W. Marshall, maintains that the schools have gone through seven rather distinct phases of development since 1900:

1. Learning only the rudiments of government. (1900)
2. Learning the government's function in social services. (1915)
3. Learning to assume responsibility for activities within the school, e.g., student government. (1920)
4. Learning that the government must correct social ills and that each citizen must want to play his part in such an endeavor. (1935)
5. Learning to take a responsible part in community activities that are quite apart from the schools, e.g., safety and clean-up campaigns. (1940)
6. Learning that good citizenship greatly depends upon the satisfaction of basic human needs and the development of a mature personality. (1945)
7. Learning that citizenship education, if it is to be effective, must

85

immediately result in certain patterns of behavior that can be seen, counted, and (hopefully in the near future) reliably scored. For this purpose, the schools have developed a list of very specific activities which must take place in a certain sequence if a child is to be ready to assume his obligations as a full citizen. (1958)[2]

Apparently, all of these changes were attempts by the school systems to make their curricula fit the specific problems of the day. However, while the public schools have shown some ability to adapt, the basic question for this study is to what extent they are influential agents of political socialization today.

Creating Loyalty

One answer to this question is provided in the work of Robert Hess and Judith V. Torney. On the basis of an impressive array of evidence, they conclude that the American public school is the single most important and effective agent in the political socialization process. Yet despite their efforts, it is still very difficult for any study to disassociate the effects of schooling from the changes that come about because of physical and cognitive maturation. As we will see, the role of the school is quite varied among different and even within the same subcultures. But before we examine these complexities, it is necessary to identify the common objectives of civics training and the core culture to which they relate.

One of the most obvious objectives of a civics program is to teach children basic concepts of loyalty, duty, and obedience. Because educators are preoccupied to a large extent with order in the school, they tend to stress rather strongly the importance of compliance to rules and authority figures. The result of this emphasis is that there is very little discussion of the individual's right to participate in social or political decision making. Because citizenship is presented in such a passive framework, the functions of political parties and interest groups are generally not discussed.

Some of the inadequacies of the civics program may be due to the fact that in many cases the teacher is unaware of the child's conceptual sophistication in dealing with politics. For example, in the later grades when the child is beginning to be more interested in political institutions, the teacher still thinks that personalities and institutions should be equally stressed. Findings such as these cast some doubt on how important the school's influence in the socialization process really is.[3]

The Textbook Democracy

Despite some disparity between a teacher's views and those of his students, by the upper elementary grades there is substantial agreement between them in many areas—especially on what constitutes a good citizen. In general, both the teacher and the children feel that a citizen should vote, obey the laws, and show an interest in his country.

Some researchers have argued that one can get an even more specific and clear-cut portrait of the good or ideal citizen by examining the major textbooks that are used in the classroom. Even today, textbooks are still significant for elementary school children and their teachers. Many of these textbooks go so far as to print in teachers' desk copies explicit statements of the values and beliefs that are supposed to be inculcated at the end of each lesson.

One of the most interesting studies of children's civics books was done by Bessie Pierce in the 1920s. She found that democracy was portrayed as being the best form of government for most of the civilized world. With such a government, liberty would be preserved under law, and the force of public opinion would be sufficiently strong to curtail any malfeasance in office. Pierce also found that these texts placed great emphasis on the deeds of military heroes and gave very little attention to more peaceful leaders, who were often discussed in rather colorless language. Her survey showed that of the 6722 lines analyzed, war heroes received 3227 lines, statesmen 1160 lines, and those engaged in enterprises of peace such as philantropists, scientists, and inventors received 2335 lines.[4]

Since the 1930s there have, of course, been significant changes in the writing and emphasis of textbooks. Generally, chauvinism and jingoistic appeals are rarely present, although history and civics books still remain favorite targets of scholars and citizens alike.[5]

There have been several more recent studies which have analyzed the values and attitudes that are presented in modern children's textbooks. One such study examined the major social studies texts intended for the third grade. This grade level is especially important for several reasons. First, it is at this level that children are exposed to an organized presentation of the community's political life. In the earlier grades, the textbooks are more oriented around the family and the neighborhood. Second, it is at this general age that children are beginning to develop a more conscious awareness of politics and political activities (Stage IV).

This study found that while there was a great emphasis on communitarian terms such as public interest, common good, and consensual politics, there was very little discussion of the possibility of political disagreement, the role of political parties, or the existence of interest groups. As might be expected, children are taught that while they should vote when they are of age, they must be guided by what is best for the whole community and not just what is in their own self-interest.

One basic problem which all Western political theory has had to deal with is how one can justify political allegiance or obligation. It is instructive to find that even children's textbooks raise this question and seek to answer it by using two different rationales. The first is that all societies, just like all children's games, have certain rules or laws which must be obeyed. If a person does not consent to obey these particular rules, then he is in effect challenging the whole fabric of law itself. The second rationale is that children receive from the government immeasurable benefits in the way of schools, health services, police and fire protection. The government has a right to expect some support from the citizens who get so much from it.

The textbooks also try to orient the child toward certain abstract political values. As might be expected, the single most frequently mentioned value is freedom or liberty, followed by fairness and toleration. Oddly enough, the type of toleration that is most often praised is *religious* toleration; there is only one mention of the more controversial and contemporary issue of racial toleration. In addition, this sample contained very few references to equality, a finding which somewhat supports Robert Lane's contention that Americans have misgivings about the desirability of a leveled society.[6]

Another way of orienting children to the political system is through the use of political symbols. It is not surprising to find that the single most frequently mentioned symbol is the American flag. The flag is the very embodiment of national pride—not just for children but for many adults as well. Also, as in the Pierce sample, these textbooks emphasize the importance of American heroes, especially George Washington. However, while there are many references to Washington and to those exemplars of American daring and enterprise—our explorers and inventors—there is very little mention of war heroes. In addition, these textbook writers apparently agree with Easton and Dennis' contention that authority figures are important sources of support for the system. Besides stressing well-known historical figures, some emphasis is placed on the policeman, the mayor, the fireman, and the President, in that order.

Lastly, the textbooks in this sample do not address themselves to complicated questions of political allegiance and participation. The good citizen is simply loyal, altruistic, informed, and concerned. The political world that he lives in is one where the government is working for the good of all, dispensing benefits from its cornucopia to the people. The citizens, both young and old, must strive to be worthy of their polity's concern.[7]

Although the above sample is rather small, James Shaver has reached similar conclusions in his review of ninety-three textbooks in American government, politics, civics, and history. While he initially examined these books to see if they stressed critical thinking, Shaver also analyzed their treatment of political topics. His most extensive examination was of American government texts, which he found quite deficient in many ways. For example, none of these books provided any method whereby a person could assess the factual claims made so often in political disputes. In addition, the treatment of propaganda was brief, and there was only cursory mention of public opinion and how it can be manipulated.[8]

The political world of the child, as presented in these textbooks, is one in which authority is benevolent and social conflict is minimal. A citizen's style of participation, then, must be dictated by the duty to put the discernible public interest above the attractions of mere selfish desires. In this way, politics becomes an intensely moral activity and the child is told that he can act with the polity in a one-to-one relationship, highly personal and always rewarding.

Of course, no analysis of civics textbooks can by itself identify the content of what is formally taught in the political socialization process. However, combined with the other findings on teacher attitudes and practices, such an analysis does enable us at least to see what ideals the school is trying to inculcate in the young. Such evidence gives us a fairly good understanding of the core concepts of civics instruction, but it does not deal with two important questions: how effective is the school in inculcating these values and how much variation is there from these core concepts in different subcultures?

The Teacher's Influence

There are many aspects of school life that could be investigated besides formal instruction: peer groups, extracurricular activities, the administrative power structure, and a score of others. But most of the attention has been devoted to the teacher and how effective he or she is in making or altering the political attitudes of students.

Except for Hess and Torney's conclusions on the primary importance of the school in political socialization, there is little evidence that the teacher's impact, by itself, is really substantial. For example, the controversial Coleman Report has found that *all* of the schools' inputs combined explain only about 10 percent of the variance in student achievement.[9] In addition, Merelman has argued that the effects of school quality on political socialization are quite limited. Another study has found that the morale of a school and the structure of the community in which students live determine attitudes more than formal instruction.[10] Even the Greeley and Rossi survey of Catholic schools concluded that without some reinforcement at home, the effects of parochial schools on religousity are minimal.[11]

Despite the bulk of evidence, it is hard to believe that teachers—especially in the elementary grades—have at best only a small impact on the attitudes of their students. It may be that the survey instruments were not sensitive enough to the possible nuances and therefore could not measure them; or it just may be that we are so used to schools which are reinforced by the family and community that the influences of the teacher, and the school in general, have never been isolated.

There is also another factor which may explain the limited effectiveness of the teacher in the classroom. This is the reluctance of many teachers to deal with politically sensitive or controversial issues.[12] Teachers as a group are rather conservative and quite self-conscious about their role. The National Education Association, for example, found that nearly two-thirds of the teachers they questioned in one survey considered themselves to be conservative. In addition, while teachers are more likely than the average citizen to participate in political and group activities, they tend to avoid organizations that are concerned with civil liberties or racial issues. Generally, they prefer the safer professional or religious associations to the more controversial advocacy groups.[13]

Even social studies teachers, who because of the nature of their subject must deal with controversial issues, tend to be rather reticent. One study done by the Survey Research Center found that a third of the social studies teachers avoided discussions of Federal aid to education, a third avoided labor-management relations, half did not discuss censorship, a fifth did not discuss communism at all, and three-quarters avoided any mention of pornography and its control.[14]

Of course, there are other types of nonpolitical, controversial issues that come up as well, e.g., evolution, sex education, and the reading of specific literary works. Here too, teachers are rather reluctant to get involved in any sort of dispute. The SRC survey of secondary school teachers of biology, English, and social studies in Michigan examined how much time was generally devoted to controversial issues.[15] The results indicate that the preponderance of teachers spent less than one-quarter of their class time on such issues.*
(See Table 6.1.)

For the purposes of this study, we are particularly interested in social

---

*One may argue that this simply reflects the fact that the established aspects of the curriculum are more important and should merit more time. But, as Massailas shows, the rest of the survey indicates that teachers are quite frequently motivated by a desire to avoid controversy in general.

Table 6.1
Percentage of Teaching Time Devoted to Controversial Issues

Percentage of teaching time	Number of teachers	Percentage of total
0-10	258	52.5
10-25	170	34.7
25-50	43	8.8
50-75	13	2.7
75-100	3	.6
No response	2	.4
	489	100.0%

Source: Reprinted by special permission from Byron-Massailas, *Education and the Political System*, p. 170, 1969, Addison-Wesley, Reading, Mass.

studies teachers who have been severly criticized by many educators for their supposed inadequacies. The first criticism is that many social studies teachers are only parttime teachers, spending the rest of their time fulfilling other duties, usually athletic coaching. It has been argued that these parttime teacher-coaches are less expressive and quite conservative in comparison to fulltime social studies teachers. However, the Survey Research Center study does not support this contention.[16]

Second, some studies have indicated that social studies teachers have a lower IQ than teachers in other fields and that this affects their ability to influence their students and present their subject matter.[17] This criticism is more difficult to deal with because it rests on the unproven assumption that effectiveness is linked to aptitude. Third, there is strong evidence that many teachers are themselves unable to distinguish conceptually between facts and values. This deficiency obviously curtails the ability of teachers, including social studies teachers, to instruct students on how to assess political and social issues.[18]

Of course, there are tremendous variations among teachers. Harmon Zeigler has found that liberal teachers are more likely to be expressive than are conservatives, and Democratic teachers are more likely to engage students in political conversations than are Republicans.[19] In addition, teachers in the big cities and in the Northeast and West are more expressive than those in small towns and in the Midwest and South.[20]

Yet overall, it does seem that many teachers are ill-prepared and not disposed to discuss controversial issues in their classrooms. Acutely aware of community and administrative pressures and employed in a highly status-conscious profession, teachers are reluctant to become too involved in disputed questions, however important they may be.

Civic Awareness

While most of the above studies do not directly explore the teacher's role in the socialization process, they do cast some doubt on whether the teacher is significantly able to mold or alter the basic political predispositions of students. However, as we have seen, the teacher and the school system are important in transmitting to children some understanding of the workings and rules of the political system. Thus, while the school may be less effective in forming attitudes of partisanship, trust, and basic morality, it is still an important agent of political socialization.

For most young children, it is the school—and probably only the school—that introduces them to politics in a formalized and structured way. The school makes its students more aware of the existence of the political system and it demands that they think about how they should relate to it. By the time students reached the end of elementary school they are beginning to enter the stage of Civic Awareness. During this stage, children learn about the functions of government and what their specific obligations are. It is no longer enough that one simply be loyal to the nation. The schools begin to stress that each citizen must have some awareness of the workings of the system and of the issues that are being discussed.

Of course, all children do not uniformly enter this stage. If the family or the community accentuates cynicism and disinterest, then it is improbable that the school can overcome this. Even if the schools in America had a common civics curriculum—which they do not—there would still be many variations in the political socialization process. As the previous chapters have indicated, black ghetto and poor white children are learning different values and have different attitudes from the middle-class children sampled. The content, and even the rate of development, is quite different across the nation. Yet even with all these obvious complications, it is interesting to find that generally for black and poor white children, the later years of school are more important. While these years are often redundant in the education of the middle class, they do enable lower status students to catch up in one sense and to acquire information about the political system which they may have missed before.[21]

This can be seen in the study done by Langton and Jennings on the importance of the civics curriculum for seniors in ninety-seven public and nonpublic schools. At first, it seems that the more civics courses a student takes, the more likely he is to be knowledgeable, to be interested, to expose himself to the political content of the media, to discuss politics, to feel efficacious, to be willing to participate, and to show tolerance. Yet when the authors examined the relationships between these attributes and the number of courses taken, they found that most of these correlations were quite trivial. In fact, considering the amount of time and money allocated for these courses, the increments are small indeed. In addition, the influence of the history curriculum is even weaker than that of the civics offerings.*

Apparently these courses have very little impact on most students in senior high school. However, there is one interesting exception—these courses do have some effect on black students. Not only do these courses provide them with basic political information, but those blacks who took such courses were much more likely to feel efficacious and tolerant than those who did not.

The civics curriculum also had some effect on attitudes toward political discussion and participation—although this effect varies with social class. Among higher status blacks, civics courses had a *negative* effect upon political discussion (and, in the South, upon political interest); among lower status blacks there was a positive effect. The same relationship occurred between participation and course taking. Apparently, the higher status black is more likely to receive from his parents a pessimistic appraisal of the possibilities of meaningful political participation and this influences how he approaches these courses. In general, though, blacks as a group tend to stress the loyalty rather than the participatory aspects of citizenship and this tendency increases with the number of courses taken.[22] (See Table 6.2.)

Passive and Active Participation

The different orientations of blacks and whites on the loyalty-participation chart is important, for it points up the fact that the same formal curriculum can be used to support varying roles. Apparently, the blacks are cognizant that their participation is less likely to be effective in the political system, and they adapt their behavioral orientations accordingly.[23]

Thus there is a great difference among school systems, with each one being surrounded by a constituent community with its own values and attitudes. What is interesting is that such variations may also be present in the same general locality. One study done by Edgar Litt in the Boston area examined three schools, each with different economic and political character-

*At this age level, there are some important increases in knowledge and interest which may be indirectly due to these courses. The next chapter discusses this aspect.

Table 6.2

Civics Curriculum and Good Citizenship Attitudes, by Race

	Number of civics courses	Loyalty	Partici-pation	Number of cases
Blacks stressing	0	51%	49%	41
	1+	75	25	85
Whites stressing	0	46	54	395
	1+	39	61	803

Source: Kenneth P. Langton and M. Kent Jennings, "Political Socialization and the High School Civics Curriculum in the United States," *American Political Science Review*, 62 (September 1968), p. 863.

istics. The first was in an upper-middle-class community with a high level of political activity; the second was in a lower-middle-class community with moderate political activity; and the third was in a working-class community with little political activity.

First, Litt did a content analysis of the civics textbooks used in each community's school over the last five years. With regard to their discussions of the democratic creed or American political institutions and procedures, there were no substantial differences. However, he did find that there were some differences when it came to discussing participation and the functions of the political system.

The texts used in working-class schools contained a few references to norms that would encourage voting, feelings of efficacy, and a sense of civic duty. Also, while the upper-middle-class school used texts that pictured politics as being a group struggle, the texts in the other two schools tended to avoid this aspect almost completely.

Litt then interviewed what he termed "potential community influentials" in order to get their views on civic education. He found that, in general, they supported the idea of inculcating basic democratic principles in children and agreed that the schools should use materials that encouraged feelings of political activity and competence in children. However, they disagreed on how politics should be presented. In the upper-middle-class community, the leaders endorsed realistic political themes which included discussions of conflict and power in the curriculum. In the other two communities there was little sympathy for this approach. These leaders wanted politics to be presented within a formal and institutional framework with emphasis on harmony rather than on struggle or conflict.

Litt concluded that each community is training its students to play different political roles. In the working-class community civic education stresses the formal aspects of government and does not spend much time on participation. In the lower-middle-class community, there is some emphasis on the responsibilities of citizenship but very little on the dynamics of decision making. In the upper-middle-class community more importance is placed on the decision-making process itself. Thus children from the latter school are being trained to be future leaders, and it is necessary that they realize, even at an early age, the complexities of the political system.[24]

By the time a student finishes secondary school, he is already being oriented toward Passive or Active Participation. At this seventh stage of development, he becomes more aware of the political process and starts to decide how he will relate to it. Joseph Adelson and his associates have found that during adolescence important changes in attitudes occur on questions of freedom, law, and community. As the adolescent grows older, he becomes more sensitive to individual freedom and the dangers of government intrusion. Youthful authoritarian attitudes are tempered by a greater degree of tolerance toward other people and groups. In addition, the adolescent is better able to conceptualize the political community and comes to understand more fully the functional nature of law and the social consequences of regulation.[25]

Other studies have indicated, however, that adolescent development may be more complex. Zellman and Sears have found that while support for freedom of speech does increase during this period, the level of support is largely dictated by one's attitudes toward the group in question, rather than by the general principle of free expression.[26]

One of the most interesting studies in this area was done by Richard Merelman. Merelman argues that while the adolescent does move from one stage of development to another, his transition is often multifaceted and uneven. Thus an individual may exhibit near "adult" characteristics in one mode of thinking, and still be less sophisticated in other modes of thinking and judgment.[27]

At any rate, whether he chooses to get involved or not, the young citizen has a certain amount of knowledge about the specific workings of politics and how it affects his life. During his school years, he is made to realize the existence of a political community, its role in the world, its functions, and lastly, its actual dynamics.

Intelligence Differences

While there are differences among communities and among school districts which affect socialization, there are variations in the classroom as well. Two of these variations have been mentioned already: sex roles and socioeconomic status. There is a third major factor that must be considered: the different intelligence levels of children in the same grades.*

In the early grades, one's basic attachment to the nation or the government is not influenced very much by intelligence levels. However, children with high IQs do tend to personalize government less and they do place greater emphasis on political institutions, such as the Supreme Court. Also, children with a higher IQ see laws as being less absolute and not always fair; they are also more impressed by the punitive powers of the government than are children with lower IQs. By the upper grade levels, these differences are more pronounced. For example, low IQ children at grade eight were as trusting in the government as were high IQ children in grades five or six.[28]

It has been found that a high IQ is positively related to feelings of efficacy, political interest, and participation.[29] Children whose scores on intelligence tests are higher are more willing to accept change, more likely to want to vote, and more frequently view themselves as being independent with regard to partisan affiliation. It also appears that the more intelligent students are less likely to hold what one study terms "Militaristic, Anti-Communist, or Super-patriotic attitudes." Such students are more committed to the Bill of Rights and are less authoritarian and more politically sophisticated. However, while high IQ students are politically more liberal, they are economically more conservative then lower IQ students.[30]

In all of these studies, researchers have held social class constant and generally found that IQ is a better predictor of political attitudes than is class. Yet there is a serious question as to whether it is statistically valid to separate two such closely related variables (such as IQ and class). The effects of these variables are so intertwined in the personalities of the individual that it is really not possible to hold one of these variables "constant." In fact, this may explain why higher IQ students are not economically more liberal even when the effects of class are supposed to be controlled.[31]

Summary

We have seen that the role of the school is too complex to isolate and analyze. Apparently, it does not upset many of the child's early predispositions toward government and authority. Yet by its formalized presentation and concern, it does devote a considerable amount of time and resources over a twelve-year period to the teaching of politics. Indeed, most of the instruction that a child gets about the system and its functions comes from the school.

*IQ scores, which are the basis for these sorts of analyses, do not really measure innate intelligence but are influenced by learned behavior and educational level.

Table 6.3
The Political Sensibility: Stages IV to VII

Manifest stage	Age	Focal point	Positive manifestation	Negative manifestation
IV. Communitarianism	7-10+	Community	Common good	Egoism
V. Abstract Allegiance	10-12	Nation-state	Unity, national primacy	Apathy
VI. Civic Awareness	12-16	Government	Beneficial functions	Cynicism
VII. Passive and Active Participation	16-18	Political process	General operational awareness	Sense of inefficacy

In addition, as the child matures, the school constantly redirects his thinking toward the life of the community and what his role in it is. At various stages in a student's life, the school seeks to reorient him into roles that are more appropriate for his age. The movement of the child through the first four stages of manifest political development is in part due to his ability to conceptualize and understand the complexities of political life. But such development is also due to the formal curricula and the efforts of the school which constantly remind the young citizen that his old ways of comprehending political reality must be altered to make way for the new. Table 6.3 summarizes these four manifest stages and their characteristics.

The relationship between the school and the maturation of the child is complex and this chapter does not seek to explain all its subtleties. What is apparent is that the child undergoes tremendous changes and that the school seeks to direct his behavior into certain modal and accepted channels. Although it is often unsuccessful, the school's objective is to give the young citizen the cognitive, social, and political skills with which he can move into adult society.

Notes

1. See Maxine Greene, *The Public School and the Private Vision* (New York: Vintage Books, 1965) and also Lawrence Cremin, *The Transformation of the School* (New York: Vintage Books, 1964).

2. Danile W. Marshall, "Citizenship: The Evolution of Educational Goals," *The Adolescent Citizen*, edited by Franklin Patterson (Glencoe, Ill.: Free Press, 1960), p. 54.

3. Robert Hess and Judith V. Torney, *The Development of Political Attitudes in Children* (New York: Anchor Books, 1967), pp. 125–129.

4. Bessie Pierce, *Civic Attitudes in American School Textbooks* (Chicago: University of Chicago Press, 1930), pp. 115–126.

5. Byron G. Massailas, "We are the Greatest," *Social Studies in the United States*, edited by C. Benjamin Cox and Byron G. Massailas (New York: Harcourt, Brace & World, 1967), pp. 167–195. Also of interest is Mark M. Krug, " 'Safe' Textbooks and Citizenship Education," *School Review* 68 (Winter 1960), 463–480.

6. Robert Lane, *Political Ideology* (New York: Free Press, 1962), pp. 57–81.

7. The complete study of third grade textbooks is in Michael P. Riccards, "Civics Books and Civic Virtue," *Child Study Journal*, II (Winter 1972), 67–74 and is discussed at greater length in Riccards, "The Concept of Participatory Citizenship: Its Philosophical Background and Systemic Importance (unpublished Ph.D. dissertation, Rutgers University, 1970), chap. 4.

8. James P. Shaver, "Reflective Thinking, Values and Social Studies Textbooks," *School Review*, 73 (Autumn 1965), 226–257.

9. James S. Coleman, et. al., *Equality of Educational* Opportunity (Washington, D.C.: Government Printing Office, 1966), p. 21. Similar findings are reported in Peter Rossi, "Social Factors in Academic Achievement," *Education, Economy and Society*, edited by A. H. Halsey, et. al. (New York: Free Press, 1961), pp. 269–272. There is, however, some evidence that certain aspects of a teacher's personality may be helpful in developing democratic attitudes. See Herbert M. Dandes. "Psychological Health and Teaching Effectiveness," *Journal of Teacher Education*, 17 (Fall 1966), 301–306.

10. Stanley E. Dimond, "Studies and Projects in Citizenship," *The Adolescent Citizen*, edited by Franklin Patterson, pp. 70–99. Richard M. Merelman, *Political Socialization and Educational Climates* (New York: Holt, 1971).

11. Andrew M. Greeley and Peter H. Rossi, *The Education of Catholic Americans* (Chicago: Aldine, 1966), pp. 219–224.

12. Harmon Zeigler, *The Political Life of American Teachers*, (Englewood Cliffs, N.J.: Prentice-Hall, 1967), pp. 118–119.

13. Cited in Byron G. Massialas, *Education and the Political System* (Reading, Mass.: Addison-Wesley, 1969), pp. 164–65.

14. Massialas, p. 172.

15. Massialas, p. 170.

16. Massialas, p. 171.

17. Martin Mayer, *Social Studies in American Schools* (New York: Harper & Row, 1962), p. 20.

18. Massailas, *Education and the Political System*, p. 179.

19. Zeigler, *The Political Life of American Teachers*, pp. 118–119.

20. M. Kent Jennings and Harmon Zeigler, "Political Expressivism among High School Teachers: The Intersection of Community and Occupational Values," *Learning About Politics*, edited by Roberta Sigel (New York: Random House, 1970), pp. 434–453.

21. See, for example, Herbert Hirsch, *Poverty and Politicization* (New York: Free Press, 1971), p. 108.

22. Kenneth P. Langton and M. Kent Jennings, "Political Socialization and the High School Civics Curriculum in the United States," *American Political Science Review*, 62 (September 1968), 852–867.

23. Langton and Jennings.

24. Edgar Litt, "Civic Education, Community Norms, and Political Indoctrination," *American Sociological Review,* 28 (February 1963), 69–75.

25. Joseph Adelson and Robert P. O'Neil, "Growth of Political Ideas in Adolescence: The Sense of Community," *Journal of Personality and Social Psychology,* 4 (1966), 295–306; Joseph Adelson, Bernard Green, and Robert O'Neil, "Growth of the Idea of Law in Adolescence," *Developmental Psychology,* 1 (1969), 327–332; Judith Gallatin and Joseph Adelson, "Legal Guarantees of Individual Freedom: A Cross-National Study of the Development of Political Thought," *Journal of Social Issues,* 27 (1971), 93–108; and Joseph Adelson and Lynnette Beall, "Adolescent Perspectives on Law and Government," *Law and Society Review,* 4 (1970), 495–504.

26. Gail L. Zellman and David O. Sears, "Childhood Origins of Tolerance of Dissent," *Journal of Social Issues,* 27 (1971), 109–136.

27. Richard M. Merelman, "The Development of Policy Thinking in Adolescence," *American Political Science Review,* 65 (December 1971), 1033–1047. Also see his *Political Socialization and Educational Climates* (New York: Holt, 1971), chap. 4.

28. Hess and Torney, *The Development of Political Attitudes,* pp. 154–169.

29. Elliot S. White, "Intelligence and Sense of Political Efficacy in Children," *Journal of Politics,* 30 (August 1968), 710–731 and his "Intelligence, Individual Differences, and Learning: An Approach to Political Socialization," *British Journal of Sociology,* 20 (March 1969), 50–68.

30. S. K. Harvey and T. G. Harvey, "Adolescent Political Outlooks: The Effects of Intelligence as an Independent Variable," *Midwest Journal of Political Science,* 14 (November 1970), 576–577.

31. Robert W. Jackman, "A Note on Intelligence, Social Class and Political Efficacy in Children," *Journal of Politics,* 32 (November 1970), 984–989. For several interesting articles on the methodological problems, see Hubert M. Blalock, Jr., "Correlated Independent Variables: The Problem of Multi-collinearity," *The Quantitative Analysis of Social Problems,* edited by Edward R. Tufte (Reading, Mass.: Addison-Wesley, 1970), pp. 418–425 and Edward R. Tufte, "Improving Data Analysis in Political Science," Tufte, pp. 437–449.

seven

An Overview of Adult Socialization

Despite the considerable amount of attention devoted to the socialization process in recent years, there are very few studies of what happens or does not happen after high school. This chapter offers some rather tentative observations about the last three stages of political socialization.

From the studies that we have examined so far, it appears that most of the major alterations in attitudes and interest come about during the elementary school years. For most people, the important changes that do take place are usually completed by the beginning of the ninth grade. In fact, relatively stable attitudes are often developed as early as the fifth grade.

While there are some increases in knowledge and sophistication during the high school years, this time is not a period of rapid growth in political interest and activity. Generally, most studies have found that political development followed one general pattern—massive and rapid growth during the elementary school years (until near adult attitudes are reached) and then a leveling off during the high school and college years into adulthood.[1] Figure 7.1 illustrates this pattern rather clearly.

Because of this presumed pattern of development, most researchers have neglected the question of adult socialization. However, one interesting exception to this state of affairs is a study done by Jennings and Niemi. While they do not deny the validity of this pattern of development, they make some major qualifications.

First, they found that there are important increases in the levels of knowledge and interest during the adolescent years. One of the main reasons

Figure 7.1
Assumed Pattern of Development of Political Attitudes and Behavior

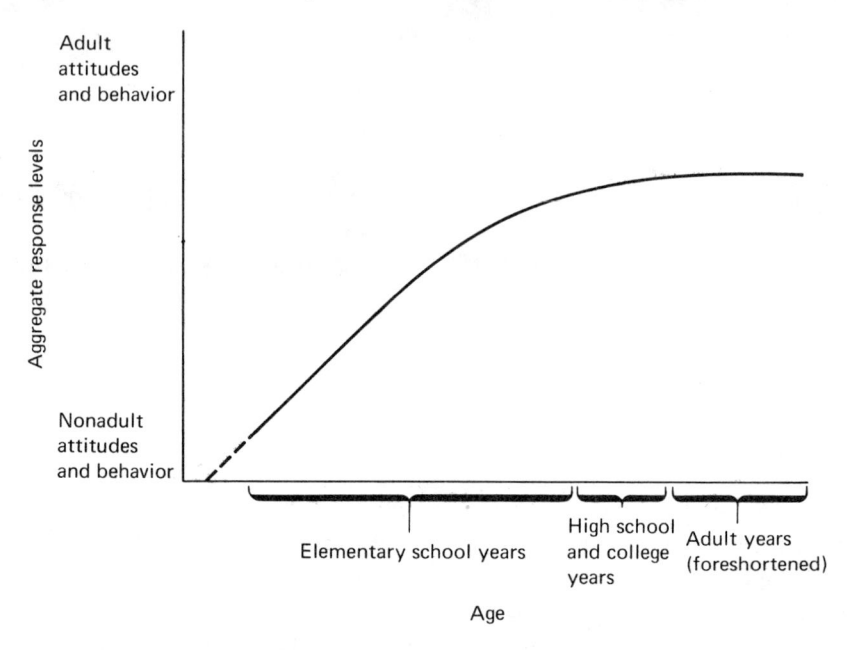

[Graph: y-axis labeled "Aggregate response levels" ranging from "Nonadult attitudes and behavior" to "Adult attitudes and behavior"; x-axis labeled "Age" with brackets for "Elementary school years," "High school and college years," and "Adult years (foreshortened)." Curve rises from low levels during elementary school years and plateaus at adult levels.]

Source: M. Kent Jennings and Richard G. Niemi, "Patterns of Political Learning," *Harvard Educational Review*, 38 (Summer 1968), p. 446. Copyright © 1968 by the President and Fellows of Harvard College.

for this may be the civics courses that are taken in high school. Even though these courses are not as effective as one would think, still about 84 per cent of the students surveyed reported that such courses increased their interest and required them to pay more attention to politics.

Second, with regard to using the media, twelfth graders are more tuned into public affairs than are younger children. Generally, while children watch television more, they pay less attention to the news than do young adults and parents. Apparently, as a person moves into adulthood he becomes more aware of the media's political offerings and is more likely to watch them. Of course, interest in politics is related to class, sex, intelligence, and education as well. Yet even with all of these factors taken into account, it is obvious that for nearly all adults regular attention to public affairs does increase above childhood levels though at varying rates.

Third, while Americans do not think very often about politics in ideological terms, the number of those who do recognize ideological differences between the parties increases during high school and early adulthood. This is another example of the increased sophistication of the young adult moving beyond his childhood attachments and feelings.

Lastly, some changes in attitudes also occur. As might be expected, there is an important increase in cynicism among the adult population which exceeds that of high school seniors. What is surprising is that there is also an interesting "regression" on the part of adults when they describe their notion of a good citizen. As we indicated in previous chapters, the young child equates the good citizen with the good man. Only as the child matures does he begin to stress the more political aspects of citizenship and the possibilities of active participation. For some reason, the adults sampled by Jennings and Niemi moved back to the moralistic aspects of citizenship by stressing that personal virtue is an important part of public duty. Also, as adults become more realistic, they become less participant oriented than are high school students who are still imbued with notions of efficacy.[2]

Thus even if we accept the idea that most of the changes that occur do so in the early stages of a person's life, there are still important qualifications to this statement. Political socialization and development does take place during adulthood. While we do not know much about these adult stages, they do at least merit brief consideration. In our typology we have already identified these adult stages; they are Preparatory Leadership, Generational Leadership, and Retrospective Leadership.

Preparatory Leadership

From the end of high school through early adulthood (ages eighteen to thirty), there occurs a time when the individual begins to become more aware of political issues and controversies. Yet, at first, he is more involved in matters of personal concern than in the public's business.[3] Although a citizen at this stage has full legal rights, he is generally far less likely to exercise his rights than his older fellow countrymen. One fairly good barometer of interest is voter turnout. The major studies in this field show that young adults are less likely to vote than any other age group. Even the elderly, with their greater propensity for illness, have a higher turnout rate.[4] (See Figure 7.2.)

However, several changes occur between eighteen and thirty. First, there is a drop in youthful apathy and disinterest. In addition, Jennings and Niemi have found that at about age thirty, there seems to take place a shift away from youthful, cosmopolitan attitudes to a more restricted perspective. This finding may be due to a generational difference: students today could just be more cosmopolitan than their elders. However, it may also be that this stage

Figure 7.2

Estimated Percentage of Eligible Population Who Voted in 1968, Divided by Age Group

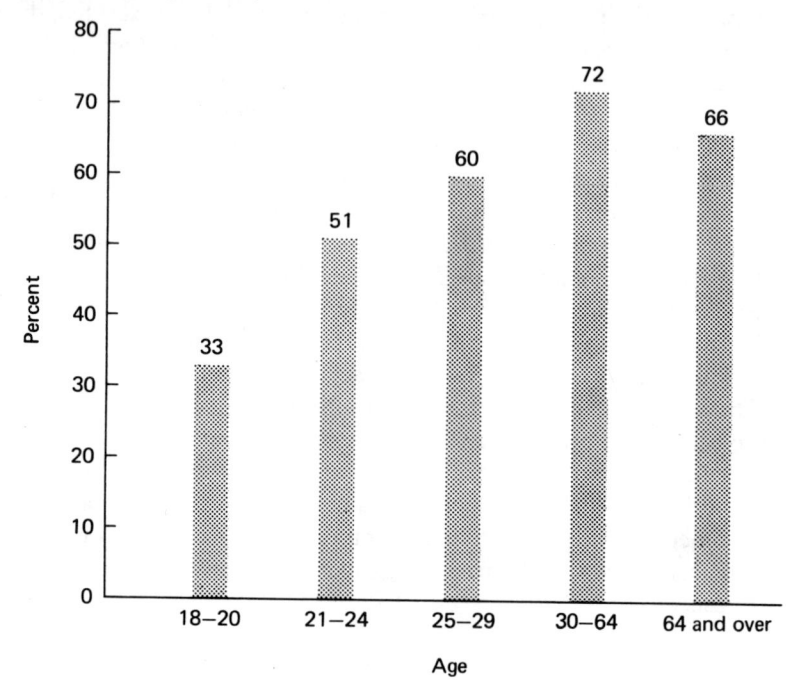

Age	Percent
18–20	33
21–24	51
25–29	60
30–64	72
64 and over	66

Source: Statistics from Richard M. Scammon and Ben J. Wattenberg, *The Real Majority* (New York: Coward-McCann, 1970), p. 48.

of adulthood is characterized by a late resurgence of nationalism and patriotic identity which is quite different from the child's early attachment to the polity.[5] If this is so then the origins of adult jingoism and the more vicious aspects of nationalistic fervor can be traced back to this stage rather than to earlier childhood inclinations. Of course, such intense political feelings can be worked out in a variety of ways—some of which may be disruptive rather than supportive of the system.

College Dissent

At this stage of development, one of the most controversial aspects of political involvement is, of course, dissent on the campus. In general, however, we have rather limited knowledge about the specific effects of college on political socialization. The popular sterotype is easier to identify—young men and women from respectable families are sent to college and are radicalized by disloyal and disenchanted professors.

The sterotype has several flaws in it. First, most professors are middle class both in their life-styles and in their political attitudes. While there is a small group of vocal dissidents (and the usual coterie of middle-aged bohemians), the political attitudes of college professors as a group can be best described as New Deal liberalism—a philosophy not very radical or even leftist after thirty-five years of temporizing and compromise. Undoubtedly, this small segment of radical professors does have some effect on a number of students, but that number is rather tiny in proportion to the millions of Americans who are exposed to college in its various shapes, sizes, and levels of quality.[6]

There have of course been many studies of the backgrounds and attitudes of campus radicals. While black radicals are easier to categorize and explain, white radical students do present some problems. Kenneth Keniston has found that white radicals usually come from fairly affluent professional backgrounds. The notion that they are revolting against the strictures of conservative parents is not true; most of their parents were liberals or socialists themselves.[7]

In addition, the highest incidence of protest activity has occurred at the major state and private universities and at prestigious liberal arts colleges. At these institutions, it was found that activists share several background characteristics: they had higher than average grades; were more academically oriented; came from secular rather than religious families; underwent democratic child-rearing practices; and were usually interested in the humanities and social sciences.

Lipset has found that these radical students, especially graduate students, often formed a natural alliance with younger assistant professors. Many of these academicians had few attachments to the universities that employed them and felt exploited in some of the same ways that the students did. These feelings were especially prevalent at the major state universities such as Berkeley, Michigan, and Wisconsin, which formed the early centers of student activity and protest. Some of the factors which led to discontent in these places were: (1) a feeling of status anxiety about oneself and about the inability of one's institution to emulate the Ivy League schools; (2) the faculty reward system, which paid extraordinary salaries to well-known scholarly luminaries and a great deal less to other professors; (3) public scrutiny or the fear of such scrutiny; (4) the proliferation of faculty committees to deal with many problems that are dealt with by administrators rather than professors in the prestigious private universities; (5) a vast bureaucracy with complicated rules and procedures; and (6) faculty preoccupation with research rather than teaching.

All of these institutional pressures created a great deal of ferment among the student body and among the less established faculty, especially in the more socially conscious disciplines. In addition, the late 1960s was a period of acute self-examination and stringent criticism. An awareness of economic inequities, a decade of intense but barely successful civil rights activism, and an unpopular war all fused together to create a weltanschauung that was accelerated by the media.[8]

However, to generalize from the 1960s would be rather misleading. Richard Flacks has argued that while the youth movement may have started with the affluent middle class, it has now spread to all segments of the postwar generation. The problem with this view is that it is not borne out in the realm of politics. For example, one of the strongest sources of support for the Wallace candidacy in 1968 was blue-collar, working-class young people. Even in the 1972 election, the liberal youth vote failed to materialize substantially. While voters under thirty were less prone to support Nixon than were their elders, the incumbent President still received about half of the youth vote. In addition, Gallup found that the vote split was roughly fifty-fifty among new voters (those from eighteen to twenty-four years old). If there is a uniformity of views within the postwar generation, it may be more in the area of social or cultural topics than in politics.

In addition, one study done by Larry Kerpelman has found that the real differences are between the activist and the nonactivist young. The activists —of the left, middle, and the right—share the same general psychological characteristics. They were found to need less support and nurturance, to value leadership more, to be more socially ascendant and assertive, and to be more sociable.[9]

The question of youthful dissent is even further complicated when one tries to assess the impact of college on students. One of the most recent and comprehensive analyses of the subject was made by Kenneth A. Feldman and Theodore M. Newcomb. Summarizing the major findings in this area, the authors concluded that freshman to senior changes did occur in several characteristics. Over the four-year span, there was a decline in authoritarianism, dogmatism, and prejudice. In addition, there was a decrease in conservative attitudes toward public policy and a growing sensitivity to aesthetic experiences. The authors did acknowledge, however, that such changes also occured in some individuals of the same age group who did not go to college, implying that maturation may have more of an effect in some cases than formal instruction.

Feldman and Newcomb also found that there was very little evidence of fraternization between students and professors. While individual faculty members are often influential, particularly with respect to career decisions, their total influence is generally not substantial.[10]

It may be more correct to argue that peer group proximity is more important in explaining political mobilization than are formal studies. Large concentrations of students with a considerable amount of leisure time have a good potential for activism. Yet, as we have seen before, such mobilization is dependent on many other variables such as family background, educational level, feelings of competence and esteem, and the general ideological climate of the time.

Generational Leadership

The period of young adulthood witnesses some important changes that lead to increases in the levels of cynicism, sophistication, and information. Gradually, from the ages twenty-five to thirty, there occurs more of an interest in politics and a greater desire for participation. At about age thirty, adults usually begin to settle down and conform to established patterns of living and social activity. Individuals undertake increasing vocational and family responsibilities which almost inevitably tie them into the day-to-day workings of society. It is obvious that people at this stage of life provide the political, economic, social, moral, and even artistic leadership of the community.

In general, the major political figures of any era are nearly all from this age group. There are, of course, notable exceptions: some may be older (as in archaic institutions such as Congress), and others may be younger. But overall, it must be remembered that youth leaders are usually mobilizing people to participate in the campaigns of middle-aged men. In the United States at least, politics is the only sport in which the major combatants are disproportionately white, middle-aged, middle-class males. From the perspectives of either endurance or wisdom, there is no evidence that this group necessarily represents a survival of the fittest. Yet is has been this group that has persistently commanded the leadership positions from one generation to another.[11]

Retrospective Leadership

If there is little research about adult socialization in general, there are even fewer studies on the changes in political behavior which accompany old age. We do know that in most occupations there is a gradual displacement of older adults which culminates in retirement, even though this cutoff point (ages sixty-two to sixty-five) probably occurs too early in life.

There have been two general explanations about how people act in these later years. The first is that old age marks a period of withdrawal from the life of the community and from occupational competition. In this way, the elderly guard themselves from social criticism and conflict by retrenching and becoming concerned with the few years of life left. The second is that this period is marked by a political conservatism which is a natural concomitant of status anxiety and economic insecurity.

It is difficult to tell if older citizens are more conservative because they have moved to the right with age or whether it is because the younger generations are just more liberal by comparison. Old-age conservatism is probably a function of both causes, although it is difficult to say so definitely. In either case, older citizens become socialized into their political roles. They come to realize that society expects certain types of behavior from them and they react accordingly by adopting one of two postures—retrospection or isolation.[12]

The posture of retrospection is an attempt by the individual to remain integrated in the community in some way. In some societies this is possible because age is associated with wisdom, but in the United States a premium is placed on youth instead. Indeed, one of the few acceptable roles for the elderly is that of grandparent. In that role it is possible for the elderly to use their experience as a comfort to the very young and their oft-repeated stories —so boring to their own children—become fresh adventures to their grandchildren.

When one looks at the frequently close union between the very young and the very old, one must be struck by the almost mystical tie that unites them. In one sense they are both free from the severe bonds of civility which often characterize social behavior. Many times, the very young and the very old seem to believe that they can be candid, honest, or even rude in a way the middle-aged would or could not be.

This orientation of retrospection has certain political consequences as well. Although the old are conservative, they seem to be conservative in a rather unique way. In the United States, few able-bodied retired people belong to political groups. Except for occasional outbursts of self-interest such as Medicare organizations, tax revolts, or the Townsend Plan in the 1930s, older people do not organize. Some of this is due to a general sort of disengagement or to personal infirmity, but it is also probably because they do not take well to mobilization.

Many times older people seem to manifest a sort of wariness that whatever is "new" has happened before. Their perspective is longer and the uniqueness of events which is so exciting to the young is absent with them. The turns of war and peace, prosperity and depression, reform and apathy are for older people part of a continuous cycle of events, while for the rest of society these occurrences are proclaimed as being bold trends or new departures.[13]

The young citizen and the old do share one common political problem:

they are both often excluded from positions of authority because of their age. Yet when they become critical of the present generation of leaders, it is from two quite different perspectives. The young dream of what could be and the elderly selectively recall what once was; consequently, no work-a-day leader can ever live up to the heroes and legends of the young and of the old.

The elderly, however, show a special concern in the need to find something to transcend death and destruction. In some cases this transcendence takes a personal and spiritual meaning; in others it means the continuation of the group after one has passed on. There are a thousand ways a man can die, but only a handful of ways he can convince himself that he can live on. It is this feeling of transcendence that explains so many aspects of our political behavior.[14] Men begin to see their lives intertwined in something greater than themselves. It is perhaps for this reason that young men go to war and old men plant trees they will never sit under.

Fitting Together

Although we have traced, in a brief way at least, the political socialization process over the whole life-cycle, it must be obvious that this description is by no means complete. For example, we have not answered what may be the most important question: how do all of these agents and variables fit together? At what level will the influence of class, education, or sex become more crucial in explaining political behavior than family upbringing? Here again our lack of a general theory is rather apparent.

There are, however, several tentative points that can be made in this regard. The first question which is usually asked is which agent is most important in the political socialization process. Hyman's early summary suggested that it is the family and many later studies have concurred.[15] However, Hess and Torney have emphasized the school and they give a respectable amount of evidence to support their conclusion.

Before we can answer this question, it is necessary to analyze just what we are asking in the first place. As we have seen, the political socialization process includes efficacy, partisanship, self-esteem, participation, ideology, interest, and many other aspects. Some agents are more important in one area than in another. The family is very strong in its ability to transmit its partisanship and in placing a child within a certain socioeconomic framework which then produces important consequences. Yet while the family is quite effective in instilling feelings of morality, efficacy, trust, and self-esteem, it is rather weak in transmitting its issue positions or ideology to its offspring.

The school plays a major role in giving students a sense of citizenship and in teaching them the formal aspects of government and politics. The media also provides information to citizens of all ages, but it is not too effective in changing their early predispositions.

Peer groups and occupational groups contribute to feelings of self-esteem and they often help to inform and mobilize people for political activity. In addition, the government itself plays a role in this complex process. A person's experiences with public agencies or leaders have an effect on his feelings of trust, efficacy, and interest. One apparatus of government, the political party system, is quite important to the socialization process because it takes complicated ideological issues and converts them into issue and leadership alternatives.

Lastly, there are also personal variables that influence the individual's political attitudes. We have seen how class, education, IQ, and—to a lesser extent—race and sex are related to feelings of efficacy, trust, and interest.

Of course, this general summary does not take into account the intensity of a person's exposure. For example, if a person is born into a high political family he may be more likely to be influenced continually by their predispositions than one who comes from an apathetic family and suddenly "discovers" politics late in life. Or if a person has been mildly inculcated into feelings of trust by the family and school and then in adolescence comes face to face with a brutal example of bureaucratic injustice, his attitudes toward authority will change considerably.

Attitude Change

A second question which must be dealt with is how and why people's attitudes and beliefs change. To what extent do events themselves cut through all of these variables and simply force the individual to reevaluate his way of thinking? People, of course, do not experience events; they experience happenings that are then put into conceptual frameworks which they already possess.

One of the most interesting phenomena to analyze is what happens when a person realizes that his interpretation of reality cannot explain particular occurrences. Basically, there are three possible alternatives: one can ignore the occurrence if it is not too important; one can seek to relate it in a distorted way to one's early preconceived notions; or one can reevaluate one's conceptual framework and either partially or totally alter it to fit the particular change.

Generally, the work of behavioral psychologists such as Leon Festinger and others has stressed how rarely people actually change their conceptual frameworks.[16] If this is so, then it means that people's basic predispositions are likely to remain the same unless they are faced with a tremendous shock, such as an economic depression or a war. In fact, the more isolated a person is geographically and intellectually, the less likely it is that he will be subjected to such shattering experiences in his lifetime.

One of the important aspects of the media—especially the electronic media—is that it barrages people with ideas, events, and values that may be at variance with a person's traditional ways of thinking. To use Festinger's terms, the media is a major source of cognitive dissonance by presenting pictures that do not fit easily into previous conceptual frameworks.

Yet even though the media has this potential, we do not actually understand its effects. Studies of films and television have been done by a variety of people mainly to see what effects pornography or violence have on children. Some of these studies are not very good and others have been affected by pressures brought by vested interests. We still do not know, for example, if frequently seeing violent acts on television over a twenty years period serves as a safety valve for violent tendencies or whether it accelerates violence. Probably, for a small group, media violence may stimulate their desire to commit real violence. For others, media violence may condition them to accept violence more often than they otherwise would. Certainly, the research of Bandura and his associates at Stanford would lend credence to the idea that television aggression and violence is likely to be imitated in real life.[17]

As for the specific effects of the electronic media on politics, we can make the following generalizations:

1. The media is an important source of information.
2. People often selectively screen out the advocacy aspects of political messages to fit their preconceived notions.
3. The caliber of political coverage in the media, especially on television, is superficial, contrived, and often attempts to stimulate controversy so as to turn the trivial into the dramatic.
4. The impressions a leader gives may be more effectively transmitted than are the contents of his speech.
5. Changes in attitudes are more likely to occur on those issues that do not directly affect an individual's personal interests. Thus a President, for example, is more likely to be able to form or change attitudes on foreign policy than on domestic policy.

Summary

This chapter has carried the political socialization process through the lifecycle. There are many areas that have not been investigated, but we have surveyed some of the relevant findings. The last three stages in our typol-

Table 7.1

The Political Sensibility: Stages VIII to X

Manifest stage	Age	Focal point	Positive manifestation	Negative manifestation
VIII. Preparatory Leadership	18-30	Political issues and controversies	Patriotic identification	Lack of identification
IX. Generational Leadership	30-60	Problem of governance	National destiny	Nonparticipation
X. Retrospective Leadership	60—	The nation in history	Transcendence and continuity	Isolation and despair

ogy were presented and they may be summarized as shown in Table 7.1.

We have also explained some of the difficulties in trying to understand how these many variables relate to one another and how attitudes are formed and altered. There are many weaknesses—both conceptual and methodological—in the study of political socialization. The next chapter critically analyzes the dimensions of these problems.[18]

Notes

1. M. Kent Jennings and Richard G. Niemi, "Patterns of Political Learning," *Harvard Educational Review*, 38 (Summer 1968), 443–446. Also of interest is Daniel Goldrich, "Political Organizations and the Politization of the Poblador," *Comparative Political Studies*, 3 (July 1970), 176–202.

2. Jennings and Niemi, "Patterns of Political Learning."

3. Erik Erikson, *Childhood and Society* (New York: Norton, 1950), pp. 227 ff.

4. Angus Campbell, et al., *The American Voter* (New York: Wiley, 1960), pp. 153–167 and William Flanigan, *The Political Behavior of the American Electorate* (Boston: Allyn and Bacon, 1968), chap. 1.

5. Jennings and Niemi, "Patterns of Political Learning," 449–450.

6. Malcolm G. Scully, "Faculty Members, Liberal on Politics, Found Conservative on Academic Issues," *The Chronicle*, 26 (April 6, 1970). This is a summary of the Carnegie Commission's survey of over 60,000 college faculty members.

7. Kenneth Keniston, *The Young Radicals* (New York: Harcourt, Brace & World, 1968).

8. S. M. Lipset and Philip G. Altbach, "Student Politics and Higher Education in the United States," *Student Politics*, edited by S. M. Lipset (New York: Basic Books, 1967), pp. 207–213.

9. Milton Mankoff and Richard Flacks, "The Changing Social Base of the American Student Movement," *The Annals*, 395 (May 1971), 54–67; also see Flacks earlier study, "The Liberated Generation: An Exploration of the Roots of Student

Protest," *Journal of Social Issues*, 22 (1967), 52–75. Kerpelman's interesting study is available in book form: *Activists and NonActivists* (New York: Behavioral Publications, 1972). Also useful is Jeanne H. Block, N. Haan, and M. B. Smith, "Socialization Correlates of Student Activism," *Journal of Social Issues*, 25 (1969), 143–177.

10. Kenneth A. Feldman and Theodore M. Newcomb, *The Impact of College on Students*, vol. 1 (San Francisco: Jossey-Bass, 1969). The effects of curriculum are discussed in Albert Somit, Joseph Tanenhaus, Walter H. Wilke, and Rita W. Cooley, "The Effect of the Introductory Political Science Course on Student Attitudes Toward Personal Political Participation," *American Political Science Review*, 52 (December 1958), 1129–1132. In addition, a variety of interpretations of student protest are presented in Julian Foster and Durward Long, *Protest: Student Activism in America* (New York: Morrow, 1970). Much of my information is from S. M. Lipset and Sheldon S. Wolin, eds., *The Berkeley Student Revolt* (New York: Anchor Books, 1965). Also of interest are Russell Middleton and Snell Putney, "Political Expression of Adolescent Rebellion," *American Journal of Sociology*, 68 (1963), pp. 527–535; Eleanor E. Maccoby, Richard E. Matthews, and Anton S. Morton, "Youth and Political Change," *Public Opinion Quarterly*, 18 (Spring 1954), pp. 23–39; and Philip Nogee and Murray Levin, "Some Determinants of Political Attitudes, among College Voters," *Public Opinion Quarterly*, 22 (Winter 1958), pp. 449–463.

11. The best summary of the kinds of people who participate in the established routes of politics is Lester W. Milbraith, *Political Participation* (Chicago: Rand McNally, 1965).

12. Wilma Donahue and Clark Tibbitts, eds., *Politics of Age* (Ann Arbor: University of Michigan, 1962).

13. Some of the information in Note 4 is quite relevant to a discussion of the attitudes of the elderly. Also see Norval D. Glenn and Michael Grimes, "Aging, Voting and Political Interest," *American Sociological Review*, (August 1968), 563–576 and John Crittenden, "Aging and Party Affiliation," *Public Opinion Quarterly*, 26 (Winter 1962), 684–657.

14. Robert Jay Lifton, *Revolutionary Immortality* (New York: Random House, 1968), explores some aspects of transcendence in Communist China. This point is also discussed in his *Boundaries* (New York: Random House, 1967).

15. Herbert Hyman, *Political Socialization* (New York: Free Press, 1959), p. 69.

16. Leon Festinger, *A Theory of Cognitive Dissonance* (Stanford: Stanford University Press, 1957) and his *Conflict, Decision and Dissonance* (Stanford: Stanford University Press, 1964). A good collection of essays on this concept is Jack W. Brechm and Arthur R. Cohen, *Explorations in Cognitive Dissonance* (New York: Wiley, 1962).

17. The controversial Surgeon General's *Report on Television and Social Behavior* (Washington, D. C.: U.S. Government Printing Office, 1971) is discussed in Robert M. Liebert and John M. Neale, "TV. Violence and Child Aggression," *Psychology Today*, 5 (April 1972), 38–40.

18. Discussions of the media's political ramifications are in Herbert Hirsch, *Poverty and Politicization* (New York: Free Press, 1971); Kurt Lang and Gladys E. Lang, *Voting and Non-Voting* (Waltham, Mass.: Blaisdell, 1968); Bernard Rubin, *Political Television, and the New Politics* (San Francisco: Chandler, 1970); and Wilbur Schram, Jack Lyle, and Edwin B. Parker, *Television in the Lives of Our Children* (Stanford: Stanford University Press, 1961).

eight

A Note on Methodology

The political socialization research done in the last decade or so has provided us with many insights and has opened up new avenues of exploration. Yet much of this research has suffered from some serious theoretical and methodological flaws. This chapter examines several of the major problems involved and how they may influence the validity of the findings we have covered.

Surveying Children

Most of the major studies in political socialization have used the techniques of survey research to find out what attitudes children have about politics and authority figures. Usually children are given written questionnaires and asked to check the responses that they consider to be most correct. However, one of the major practitioners of this method, Roberta Sigel, has pointed out some of the complications of using the survey method with children.

First, some children (especially teenagers) may not take the questionnaire seriously. Second, boys and girls often tend to regard the questionnaire as a "test" and they are more likely to choose the answer they feel is correct rather than the one that most closely coincides with their feelings. Third, the questionnaire by its very phraseology may be eliciting a specific response.

For example, Sigel used the Hess-Easton items to see if the children in her sample idealized the President. She found that they answered that the Chief Executive was more hard-working, more reasonable, and more knowledgeable about politics. But when she orally interviewed these children (ages ten to fourteen), she found that the logic used in arriving at these answers was quite involved. While the children answered that the President was rather reasonable, they thought this was due to the fact that he had to be in order to work with Congress and with the other people in government. He knew more because he had many advisors and experts and because politics was his business. Sigel observed that "a President who is responsive to people because he wants to get re-elected is not the same as a President who is responsive because he is a superior human being. . . . Certainly these answers do not point to unadultered idealization. If we deal with idealization at all, it is idealization tempered by realism." Overall, Sigel found that the congruence between oral interviews and structured questionnaires was rather low.[1]

Even survey research done with adults reveals some serious problems. For example, Richard Niemi has matched students with their parents and husbands with their wives and then compared all responses on virtually identical questions. He found that on questions of family structure and interaction, there was little agreement among the respondents. On political questions and evaluations of sociopolitical groups, there was at best only a moderate amount of correspondence. This means that much of the information on the family characteristics and attitudes may be inaccurate because it is usually based on only one person's responses.[2]

In addition, John Wahlke and Milton Lodge have speculated that there is a difference between the way people feel about issues and what they say or even think they feel. By using a polygraph machine, these two political scientists have tested the correspondence between psychophysiological responses and verbal self-reports and they have found significant discrepancies. Their early experiments must lead one to question seriously survey research methodology.[3]

Obviously, these problems become even more apparent when dealing with children. If there were no other difficulties, researchers would still have to be careful to use terms which have the same meaning for all children. For example, the previous chapters have examined the child's differing views of the good citizen. However, Sigel found that the term *citizenship* is used in today's schools as a synonym for conduct. Thus a well-behaved pupil is termed a good citizen; it is not surprising that the child associates citizenship with obeying the school's rules and regulations.[4]

Differences in Development

Besides these methodological problems, there are more basic questions that arise as well. The foremost one is why we are interested in children's attitudes in the first place. The answer that is usually given is that it is *assumed* that by understanding the patterns of childhood development we can comprehend why adults act the way they do. As we have seen, there are a great many qualifications to this view—especially if one views political socialization as a lifelong process.

In order to deal with this development, most studies in political socialization have examined students at different grade levels. The differences between the children in grade three and those in grade eight are seen as constituting a pattern of development—but this is not necessarily so. Such a view completely screens out the influence of the social environment and its controversies. Sigel has posed one rather good example of this problem. If fourth graders answer that protest and marches are a legitimate form of citizen activity, and eighth graders mention voting and letter writing instead, are we correct in assuming that as children grow older they disavow more militant methods for the conventional ones? Does it not make more sense to recognize that the younger children have grown up in an era when protest is rather common, while older children may still remember when these sorts of occurrences were shocking? The point is that one can only identify developmental patterns by following the *same* people over a long period of time. The other method is adopted because it is easier, cheaper, and quicker for the purposes of the investigators.[5]

This question of development leads us into another difficulty. It makes sense for us to examine differences in childhood political attitudes if they carry over in some form into adulthood. However, if we find, for example, in later studies that black elementary school children are more cynical than white elementary school children, but that by age eighteen they reach the same level of cynicism, what have we learned? Such findings would tell us much about individual and group rates of development, but they do not explain graphically the relationship between the socialization process and the political system.

Also, in analyzing these differences in development, a considerable amount of emphasis has been placed on variables such as class, IQ, sex, religion, and ethnicity. The standard statistical method is to isolate one variable and control the others to find out if the first variable has a high correlation with the item in question. For example, some of these studies have tried to do this with IQ and political attitudes by controlling socioeconomic status; but while it is statistically possible to do this, it is probably not methodologically valid. As Blalock has pointed out, "when the correlation between two or more independent variables is high, the sampling error of the partial slopes and partial correlations will be quite large."[6]

Attitudes and Nonattitudes

At several points in this study, we have noted the difficulty in trying to assess the exact significance of all of these variables and explain in a systemic way how the political socialization process works. Some of the answer as to *how* lies in the normal development of a person throughout the life cycle. Yet no typology is a substitute for a general theory—it is merely a first step in its formulation.

One of the roadblocks to a development of a theory of political socialization has been the uncertain state of personality research. Theories and findings abound, but there is no systematic framework that explains the workings of psychological man. In trying to comprehend how and why people adopt the political attitudes they do, we run head on into this roadblock—and a related one of our own.

For decades, political science and psychology have accepted one general idea—that there is an underlying personality which is more or less stable regardless of the situation. If we only understood the forces that created this personality, then we could explain an individuals' behavior. However, the work of Walter Mischel and other psychologists does not support this view at all. They argue that there is little evidence of consistency in behavior; for example, a person who is rigid in one area may be flexible in another, or one who is politically liberal may be socially conservative. Attitudes change with the type of situation one is faced with, and, in making value judgments, individuals do not move from principles to specifics very often.

One of the most interesting studies of this question was done by Hartshorne and May in the 1920s. In analyzing how children make moral decisions, they found that children vary their opinions to fit the situation and that they do not exhibit a general code of morals. On the basis of this study and a great deal more recent ones, Mischel argues that there is little evidence of a superego or a unitary intrapsychic moral agency. Moral judgments and verbal standards of right and wrong, resistance to temptation, and indices of guilt and remorse are not interrelated.[7] Thus it seems that in trying to explain political behavior, political scientists may have over-simplified stabilities and continuities in personality.

In fact, political scientists are in an even more precarious position than psychologists in this regard. For quite a few years, political scientists have assumed that people did at least think about politics. However, there is increasing evidence that they may be forcing people with no attitudes to choose some attitudes for the purposes of answering survey questions.

One of the major investigators of this problem, Philip Converse, has examined the belief systems of mass publics and he has found results rather similar to those of Mischel. Converse could discover very little consistency or functional interdependence in these belief systems.[8] In a later paper, Converse maintained that a large proportion (close to 50 percent) of the respondents in national surveys really do not have any attitudes at all on many political questions. Yet most adults, like most children, approach attitude questionnaires as if they were intelligence tests and they are reluctant to indicate they may not "know" the answer.[9]

If there is a considerable number of adults who do not really possess political attitudes, how much higher is the percentage among children? It may be that politics is an area of endeavor about which the young know a little, but in which they just are not too interested until some adult imposes them and demands that they respond to political events and questions in a demonstrable way. If this is so, children may be simply telling us what they think we want them to say without really "feeling" or incorporating these ideas into their attitudinal framework.[10] In fact, at least one study of children's political attitudes indicates just that. In her research of 1000 elementary school students in the Berkeley-Oakland area, Pauline Vaillancourt found that there was very little continuity in the children's answers from one test to another. Instead of using the usual explanation that the survey tools were inadequate, Vaillancourt indicates that her sample may just not have developed stable political attitudes.[11]

Summary

At first glance, it may seem as if all these problems make past research meaningless and further research impossible. Yet this impression would be a mistake; the studies that we have examined have provided us with a vast collection of insights and testable hypotheses. Most important, they have resurrected an old field of inquiry and breathed a little empirical life into it.

However, in the future it will be necessary to test our hypotheses on cross-cultural samples and to conduct indepth personal interviews to supplement the paper and pencil questionnaires. Most of all, we must undertake longitudinal studies which allow us to follow individuals as they progress through the life cycle and are affected by the process of aging and by the catalyst of events.

Notes

1. Roberta Sigel, "Political Socialization: Some Reflections on Current Approaches and Conceptualizations," (A paper delivered at the American Political Socialization Association Convention, September 6–10, 1966).

2. Richard Niemi, "Reliability and Validity of Survey and Non-Survey Data About the Family," (A Paper delivered at the American Political Science Association Convention, September 7–11, 1971).

3. John Wahlke and Milton Lodge, "Psychophysiological Measures of Change in Political Attitudes," (A paper delivered at the Midwest Political Science Association Convention, April 28 - May 1, 1971).

4. Sigel, "Political Socialization," p. 9. A more flexible and open method of interviewing is advocated in Fred I. Greenstein and Sidney Tarrow, "Political Orienta-

tions of Children: The Use of a Semi-Projective Technique in Three Nations," (Beverly Hills: Sage Publications, 1970).

5. Sigel, "Political Socialization," p. 3. Kenneth Prewitt, George von der Muhel, and David Court, "School Experiences and Political Socialization' A Study of Tanzanian Secondary School Children," *Comparative Political Studies*, 3 (July 1970), 203–225 make the point that childhood changes cannot simply be ascribed to age. They argue that age is not an independent variable, but a surrogate variable for different socialization experiences.

6. Hubert M. Blalock, Jr., "Correlated Independent Variables: The Problem of Multicollinearity," *The Quantitative Analysis of Social Problems*, edited by Edward R. Tufte (Reading, Mass.: Addison-Wesley, 1970), p. 418.

7. Walter Mischel, *Personality and Assessment* (New York: Wiley, 1968), chap. 2.

8. Philip Converse, "The Nature of Belief Systems of the Mass Public," *Ideology and Discontent*, edited by David E. Apter (New York: Free Press, 1964), pp. 206–261.

9. Philip Converse, "Attitudes and Non-Attitudes: Continuation of a Dialogue," Tufte, *The Quantitative Analysis of Social Problems*, pp. 168–189.

10. These problems are explored in William R. Schonfeld's interesting review article, "The Focus of Political Socialization Research: An Evaluation," *World Politics* 23 (April 1971), 544–578.

11. Pauline M. Vaillancourt, "The Stability of Children's Political Orientations," *Public Opinion Quarterly* (forthcoming).

Bibliographical Essay

The literature on the topic of political socialization is immense, especially if one includes relevant works in other disciplines. For those who are interested in investigating a particular topic in greater depth, the following list may be of some help. More comprehensive lists of references are contained in the notes at the end of each chapter.

The major works on political socialization are Herbert Hyman, *Political Socialization* (Glencoe, Ill.: Free Press, 1959); David Easton and Jack Dennis, *Children in the Political System* (New York: McGraw-Hill, 1969); Robert Hess and Judith V. Torney, *The Development of Political Attitudes in Children* (New York: Anchor Books, 1967); Kenneth P. Langton, *Political Socialization* (New York: Oxford University Press, 1969); Fred I. Greenstein, *Children and Politics* (New Haven: Yale University Press, 1965); Richard E. Dawson and Kenneth Prewitt, *Political Socialization* (Boston: Little, Brown, 1969); Robert E. Cleary, *Political Education in the American Democracy* (Scranton: Intext Educational Publishers, 1971); Charles F. Andrian, *Children and Civic Awareness* (Columbus, Ohio: Charles E. Merrill Books, Inc., 1971); and Herbert Hirsch, *Poverty and Politicization* (New York: Free Press, 1971). Still of use is Charles Merriam's seminal work, *The Making of Citizens* (Chicago: University of Chicago Press, 1931).

Except for Langton's work, these studies all concentrate on the United States. There are a number of works on other nations as well: Stephen A. Douglas, *Political Socialization and Student Activism in Indonesia* (Urbana: University of Illinois Press, 1970); Urie Bronfenbrenner, *Two Worlds of Childhood: U. S. and U. S. S. R.* (New York: Russell Sage Foundation, 1970); Edward Banfield, *The Moral Basis of a Backward Society* (New York: Free

Press, 1958); Lucian Pye's two interesting volumes, *Politics, Personality and Nation Building* (New Haven: Yale University Press, 1962) and *The Spirit of Chinese Politics* (Cambridge, Mass.: MIT Press, 1968); Richard Wilson, *Learning to Be Chinese* (Cambridge, Mass.: MIT Press, 1970); Laurence Wylie, *Village in the Vaucluse,* revised edition, (Cambridge, Mass.: Harvard University Press, 1964); and an interesting review article by Fred I. Greenstein and Sidney G. Tarrow, "The Study of French Political Socialization: Toward the Revocation of Paradox," *World Politics,* 22 (October 1969), 95–138.

Two good collections of monographs are Roberta Sigel, ed., *Learning About Politics* (New York: Random House, 1970) and Norman Adler and Charles Harrington, eds., *The Learning of Political Behavior* (Glenview, Ill.: Scott, Foresman, 1970). Scholarly journals frequently devote a whole issue to political socialization, such as *Social Science Quarterly* (September 1968); *Harvard Educational Review* (Summer 1968); *The Annals of the American Academy of Political and Social Science* (September 1965 and May 1971); *Comparative Education Review* (June 1966); *Comparative Political Studies* (July 1970); *Daedalus* (Winter 1968 and Fall 1971); and *Journal of Social Issues* (October 1964 and July 1967).

The superb studies of Jean Piaget and his associates span several decades and are incorporated in a variety of monographs, a few of which are: *The Moral Judgment of the Child* (New York: Free Press, 1965); *The Psychology of Intelligence* (Totawa: Littlefield, Adams, 1950); *Judgment and Reasoning in the Child* (New York: Humanities Press, 1952); *The Origins of Intelligence in Children* (New York: International Universities Press, 1952); and *Six Psychological Studies* (New York: Random House, 1967).

Piaget's insights have been developed and enlarged upon by many other investigators, most notably Lawrence Kohlberg. Kohlberg's analysis can be found in David Goslin, ed., *Handbook of Socialization Theory and Research* (Chicago: Rand McNally, 1969) and in Martin L. Hoffman and Lois W. Hoffman, eds., *Review of Child Development,* vol. I (New York: Russell Sage Foundation, 1964). One political scientist who has expressed considerable interest in Piaget's work is Richard M. Merleman in "The Development of Political Ideology," *American Political Science Review,* 63 (September 1969), 750–67.

Much of the work in child psychology is relevant to political socialization. The studies done by Jerome Kagan are of a consistently high caliber. See Kagan and Howard A. Moss, *Birth to Maturity* (New York: Wiley, 1962). Albert Bandura and Richard Walters, *Social Learning and Personality Development* (New York: Holt, 1963) is also quite pertinent. The very complex problem of defining personality is dealt with rather well in Laurence A. Pervin, *Personality: Theory, Assessment and Research* (New York: Harcourt, Brace & World, 1969).

Child-rearing practices are discussed in John W. M. Whiting and Irving Child, *Child Training and Personality* (New Haven: Yale University Press, 1953); Robert R. Sears, Eleanor E. Maccoby, and Harry Levin, *Patterns of Child Rearing* (Evanston, Ill.: Row, Peterson, 1957); and Frank Estvan and Elizabeth Estvan, *The Child's World* (New York: Putnam, 1959).

There are many treatments of the social forces that influence children. Two of the best discussions on sex differences are Eleanor E. Maccoby, ed., *The Development of Sex Differences* (Stanford: Stanford University Press, 1966) and Harriet Holter, *Sex Role and Social Structure* (Oslo: Universitietsforlaget, 1970). Class differences are explored in Donald G. McKinley, *Social Class and Family Live* (New York: Free Press, 1964); Richard Centers, *The Psychology of Social Classes* (Princeton: Princeton University Press, 1949); and Alan L. Grey, *Class and Personality in Society* (New York: Atherton, 1969).

Ethnic group differences are discussed in Nathan Glazer and Daniel P. Moynihan, *Beyond the Melting Pot* (Cambridge, Mass.: MIT Press, 1966); Edgar Litt, *Beyond Pluralism* (Glenview, Ill.: Scott, Foresman, 1970); Milton Gordon, *Assimilation in American Life* (New York: Oxford University Press, 1964); Herbert Gans, *The Urban Villagers* (New York: Free Press, 1962); and two interesting anthologies, one by Lawrence H. Fuchs, ed., *American Ethnic Politics* (New York: Harper & Row, 1968) and the other by Harry A. Bailey, Jr. and Ellis Katz, eds., *Ethnic Group Politics* (Columbus, Ohio: Charles E. Merrill Books, Inc., 1969). The political implications of religious affiliation are explored in Gerhard Lenski, *The Religious Factor* (New York: Anchor Books, 1963).

Peer group activity has been examined by a variety of researchers, usually, however, with little emphasis on political behavior. Some studies of interest are James Samuel Coleman, *The Adolescent Society* (New York: Free Press, 1961); H. H. Remmers and D. H. Radler, *The American Teenager* (Indianapolis: Bobbs-Merrill, 1957); Elizabeth Douvan and Joseph Adelson, *The Adolescent Experience* (New York: Wiley, 1966); and Samuel Eisenstadt, *From Generation to Generation* (Glencoe, Ill.: Free Press, 1956).

One of the recent subfields in political science is the politics of education. Many of its findings are very relevant to any study of the role of the school in political socialization. An interesting overview is Byron M. Massailas, *Education in the Political System* (Reading, Mass.: Addison-Wesley, 1969). Other studies in this area are Robert M. Merelman, *Political Socialization and Educational Climate* (New York: Holt, 1971); Robert E. Agger and Marshall Goldstein, *Who Will Rule the Schools* (Belmont, Calif.: Wadsworth, 1970); Philip Meranto, *School Politics in the Metropolis* (Columbus, Ohio: Charles E. Merrill Books, Inc., 1970); Louis Masotti, *Education and Politics in Suburbia* (Cleveland: Western Reserve University Press, 1967); Nicholas Masters, et al., *State Politics and the Public Schools* (New York: Knopf, 1964); Stephen Bailey, et. al., *Schoolmen and Politics* (Syracuse: Syracuse University Press, 1962); and Alan Rosenthal's *Pedagogues and Power* (Syracuse: Syracuse University Press, 1969) and his anthology, *Governing Education* (New York: Anchor Books, 1969).

More critical discussions of American education are numerous and include Edgar Friedenberg, *Coming of Age in America* (New York: Knopf, 1965); Paul Goodman, *Growing Up Absurd* (New York: Vintage Books, 1960); and Charles Silberman, *Crisis in the Classroom* (New York: Random House, 1970). The best discussion of Catholic schools is by Andrew Greeley and Peter Rossi, *The Education of Catholic Americans* (Chicago: Aldine, 1966).

Various aspects of college education are discussed in: Clark Kerr, *The Uses of the University* (Cambridge, Mass.: Harvard University Press, 1963); David Riesman, *Constraint and Variety in American Education* (New York: Doubleday, 1958); S. M. Lipset and Sheldon Wolin, eds., *The Berkeley Revolt* (New York: Anchor Books, 1965); Nevitt Sanford, *The American College* (New York: Wiley, 1962); Daniel Bell and Irving Krostol, eds., *Confrontation: The Student Rebellion and the Universities* (New York: Basic Books, 1969); Lewis S. Feuer, *The Conflict of Generations* (New York: Basic Books, 1969); William P. Gerberding and Duane E. Smith, eds., *The Radical Left: The Abuse of Discontent* (Boston: Houghton Mifflin, 1970); Paul Jacobs and Saul Landau, eds., *The New Radicals* (New York: Random House, 1966); and a comprehensive bibliography by Kenneth Keniston and Michael Lerner, "Selected References on Student Protest," *The Annals*, 395 (May 1971), 184–94.

There is very little data on adult political socialization. Probably the best information can be extrapolated from studies of political behavior and public opinion. Some of the major works are: S. M. Lipset, *Political Man* (New York: Anchor Books, 1960); Lester Milbraith, *Political Participation* (Chicago: Rand McNally, 1965); V. O. Key, *Public Opinion and American Democracy* (New York: Knopf, 1961); Gabriel Almond and Sidney Verba, *The Civic Culture* (Princeton: Princeton University Press, 1963); Lloyd A. Free and Hadley Cantril, *The Political Beliefs of Americans* (New Brunswick, N. J.: Rutgers University Press, 1968); and Robert Lane's trilogy, *Political Life* (New York: Free Press, 1959), *Political Ideology* (New York: Free Press, 1962), and *Political Thinking and Consciousness* (Chicago: Markham, 1970).

The most sophisticated opus on political behavior is in the area of voting studies. The older works are Paul Lazarsfeld, Bernard Berelson, and Hazel Gaudet, *The People's Choice* (New York: Duell, Sloan & Pearce, 1944) and Bernard Berelson, Paul F. Lazarsfeld, and William N. McPhee, *Voting* (Chicago: University of Chicago Press, 1954). The basic work is done now by the Survey Research Center at the University of Michigan. See Angus Campbell, Gerald Gurin, and Warren Miller, *The Voter Decides* (Evanston, Ill.: Row, Peterson, 1954), and Angus Campbell, Philip Converse, Warren Miller, and Donald Stokes, *The American Voter* (New York: Wiley, 1960) and their *Elections and the Political Order* (New York: Wiley, 1966). *The American Political Science Review* usually contains SRC analyses of the national elections which supplement these other volumes. Also of interest are V. O. Key, *The Responsible Electorate* (Cambridge, Mass.: Harvard University Press, 1966); William Flanigan, *Political Behavior of the American Electorate* (Boston: Allyn and Bacon, 1968); and Gerald M. Pomper, *Elections in America* (New York: Dodd, Mead, 1970).

Two good introductions to a study of adult attitudes are David Sears and Robert Lane, *Public Opinion* (Englewood Cliffs, N. J.: Prentice-Hall, 1964) and Bernard Hennessy, *Public Opinion* (Belmont, Calif.: Wadsworth, 1971). Important articles are contained in the anthologies by Edward C. Dreyer and Walter A. Rosenbaum, eds., *Political Opinion and Behavior* (Belmont, Calif.: Wadsworth, 1970) and Nelson Polsby, Robert Dentler, and Paul Smith, eds., *Politics and Social Life* (Boston: Houghton Mifflin, 1963).

There are some interesting studies of occupational socialization: Everett C. Hughes, *Men and Their Work* (Glencoe, Ill.: Free Press, 1958); Anselm L. Strauss, *Mirrors and Masks* (Glencoe, Ill.: Free Press, 1959); Morris Janowitz, *The Professional Soldier* (Glencoe, Ill.: Free Press, 1960); and Erving Goffman's perceptive *Asylums* (New York: Doubleday, 1961). Some parts of Orville G. Brim, Jr. and Stanton Wheeler, *Socialization After Childhood: Two Essays* (New York: Wiley, 1966) are also quite useful.

While the specific topic of political socialization after high school has not been investigated much, a few relevant exceptions are: M. Kent Jennings and Richard G. Niemi, "Patterns of Political Learning," *Harvard Educational Review*, 38 (Summer 1968), 443–67; S. M. Lipset, ed., *Student Politics* (New York: Basic Books, 1967); and Wilma Donahue and Clark Tibbitts, eds., *Politics of Age* (Ann Arbor: University of Michigan Press, 1962).

The relationship between television and politics is explored in Bernard Berelson and Morris Janowitz, eds., *Reader in Public Opinion and Communication* (New York: Free Press, 1966); Bernard Rubin, *Political Television* (Belmont, Calif.: Wadsworth, 1967); and Wilbur Schram, Jack Lyle, and Edwin B. Parker, *Television in the Lives of Our Children* (Stanford: Stanford University Press, 1961).

Political science methodology has been the subject of many studies. Some of the more interesting ones are Oran R. Young, *Systems of Political Science* (Englewood Cliffs, N. J.: Prentice-Hall, 1968); Philip G. Zimbardo and Ebbe E. Ebbesen, *Influencing Attitudes and Changing Behavior* (Reading, Mass.: Addison-Wesley, 1969); and Charles Y. Glock, *Survey Research in the Social Sciences* (New York: Russell Sage Foundation, 1967).

Index

Abstract Allegiance, 18, 74, 76, 81, 87
Adelson, Joseph, 11, 59, 95
Adorno, T.W., 36
Adult socialization, 2, 9, 15, 18-19, 101-119
Aggression, 35-36, 38, 55
Almond, Gabriel, 10
Aristotle, 5, 7, 11
Assimilation, 23
Attitudes:
    and nonattitudes, 117-119
    change, 110-111
Authoritarianism, 26, 36-37, 43, 57, 63, 95-96, 106
Authority, 2, 13, 17, 28, 58, 69, 70-73, 76, 81, 86, 96, 110

Bandura, Albert, 35, 111
Benevolence, 76, 81
Blacks, 61-62, 64, 78-81, 92-93, 105
Blalock, Hubert M., Jr., 117
Bronfenbrenner, Urie, 59

Campbell, Angus, 54
Catholics, 61-63 (see also Schools)
Child, Irving, 38

Child-rearing practices, 10 (see also Class)
Civic Awareness, 18, 92-93
Class, 12, 56-62, 76-81, 92-96, 102, 105-107, 109-110, 117
    and child discipline, 37-38, 42
    and child-rearing patterns, 38, 56-57, 105
    and political recruitment, 46-47
Cognitive dissonance, 110-111
Coleman, James S., 59-60, 89
Collective monologues, 27
College youth, 60, 104-107
Command Morality, 16, 27-28, 73
Communitarianism, 18, 69, 87-88
Community, 2, 28, 69-81, 95
Congress, 70, 73, 107, 116
Conscience, 28, 37-38
Consensus Morality, 16, 28-29, 71
Converse, Philip, 118
Coward, Noel, 9
Cynicism, 14, 16, 36, 39, 81, 92, 103, 117

Democracy, 73, 87, 94
Dennis, Jack, 11, 70-71, 88
Dewey, John, 11, 85

127

Douvan, Elizabeth, 59
Duty, 30, 86, 103
Duverger, Maurice, 54

Easton, David, 11, 70-71, 88, 115
Education, 40, 43-45, 54-55, 92, 109-110 (see also Schools)
Efficacy, 10, 23, 25-26, 36, 42-43, 48, 54, 74, 81, 93-94, 96, 103
Epperson, D.C., 60
Equality, 29, 30, 73, 88
Erikson, Erik, 11, 25, 36
Ethnicity, 2, 61-66, 117 (see also Blacks; Catholics; Jews; Protestants)

Fairness, 23, 73
Family, 2, 7, 12-13, 16, 23, 35-48, 69, 78, 107, 109-110, 116
   authoritarian, 40-42
   issue transmittal, 47-48
   maternal, 42-43
   partisanship, 40, 43-45, 48
   political recruitment, 46-47
   power structure, 40, 42-43, 57, 116
Faulkner, William, 38
Feldman, Kenneth A., 106
Festinger, Leon, 110-111
Flacks, Richard, 106
Flag, 88
Freud, Sigmund, 38

Gallup poll (1972), 106
Generational conflict, 59-60
Generational Leadership, 18-19, 103-107
Good citizen, the, 10, 73, 103, 116
Government, concept of, 13, 18, 69-70, 73, 80-81, 88, 96
Greeley, Andrew, 63, 90
Greenberg, Edward, 79

Greenstein, Fred I., 11, 55, 57
Guilt, 23, 37-39

Hartshorne, H., 118
Hawthorne, Nathaniel, 38
Hess, Robert, 11, 73, 86, 89, 115
Hirsch, Herbert, 78
Hobbes, Thomas, 11
Hyman, Herbert, 12

Identification, 35, 37 (see also Models)
Intelligence Quotient (IQ), 12, 91, 95-96, 102, 110, 117-118
Imitation, 16, 24-27, 35, 69

Jaros, Dean, 76
Jennings, M. Kent, 11, 45, 92, 101, 103
Jews, 61-63
Justice, 29-30

Keniston, Kenneth, 105
Kennedy brothers, assassinations of, 39
Kerner Commission, 39
Kerpelman, Larry, 106
King, Martin Luther, Jr., 39
Kohlberg, Lawrence, 30-31

Lane, Robert, 57, 88
Langton, Kenneth P., 11, 40-41, 45, 60, 92
Lasswell, Harold, 26*n*
Latent stages, 15
Laws, 18, 28, 70, 73, 88, 95 (see also Rules)
Learning, types of, 7
Lipset, Seymour Martin, 36-37, 57, 105
Litt, Edgar, 11, 93-95

Lodge, Milton, 116
Loyalty, 86, 92-93
Lyons, Schley, 81

McCarthy, Eugene, 60
McGovern, George, 60
Machiavelli, Niccolo, 11
Manifest stages, 15, 97
Mann, Horace, 85
Marshall, Daniel W., 85
Massailas, Byron G., 90
May, M.A., 118
Media, 2, 13, 78, 93, 102, 109-111
Melville, Herman, 38
Merelman, Richard M., 89, 95
Merriam, Charles, 11
Methodological problems, 2, 115-119
Mischel, Walter, 118
Modal personality, 10
Models, 16, 24, 35 (see also Identification)
Morality, 2, 28, 30-31, 48, 75, 92, 103
Motive, 29

National character, 9, 11-12
National Education Association, 90
Newcomb, Theodore M., 106
Niemi, Richard G., 101, 103, 116
Nixon, Richard M., 60, 106

Obedience, 86
Obligation, 27, 30, 88

Paideia, 11
Parties, political, 11, 87-88, 110
Partisanship, 36, 43-45, 75, 78, 92, 96, 109 (see also Family)
Passive and Active Participation, 18, 95

Peer group, 2, 12-13, 40, 58, 61, 69, 78, 106-107, 110
Physiological development, 15, 58, 86
Piaget, Jean, 2, 24-31
Pierce, Bessie, 87-88
Plato, 11
Policeman, 70-71, 73, 79, 88
Political recruitment (see Class; Family)
Political sensibility, 2
Political socialization, 1
   and immigrants, 8
   and the life cycle, 1, 14, 37, 117-119
   areas of research, 12
   definition of, 8
   history of its study, 11-16
   typology of, 14, 16-19
Politics:
   as symbolism, 1, 7, 11
   definition of, 7
Preparatory Leadership, 18, 103-107
President, 7, 70-79, 88, 115-116
Prewitt, Kenneth, 46
Protestants, 61-63
Psychological development, 30, 36
Punishment, 29-30, 35, 37, 61

Race, 2, 110 (see also Blacks)
Radler, D.H., 60
Reinforcement, 25
Religion, 12, 40, 117 (see also Catholics; Jews; Protestants)
Remmers, H.H., 60
Responsibility, 18, 29
Retrospective Leadership, 19, 103, 107-109
Rossi, Peter, 63, 90
Rousseau, Jean Jacques, 11
Rules, 16, 26, 28-29, 58, 73, 86, 88 (see also Laws)

Schools, 11, 13, 18, 58, 74, 85-97, 101-102, 109
    Catholic, 90
    purposes of, 85-86
Sears, David O., 95
Self-esteem, 2, 23, 26, 35, 48, 69, 109
Sex role, 2, 12, 53-58, 95, 102, 109-110, 117
Shakespeare, William, 6
Shaver, James, 89
Sigel, Roberta S., 11, 115-117
Socialization:
    definition of, 5
    extent of, 5-7
    (*see also* Political socialization)
Supreme Court, 73, 96

Teachers, 86-91, 105-106
Textbooks, 86-89
Tolerance, 35, 88, 93, 95

Torney, Judith V., 11, 73, 86, 89
Toynbee, Arnold, 24-25
Trust, 2, 10, 14, 16, 23, 25-26, 35-36, 48, 69, 71, 73, 76, 92, 109-110

Vaillancourt, Pauline M., 119
Verba, Sidney, 10
Voting, 1, 54, 62, 73-74, 78, 87, 94

Wahlke, John, 116
Wallace, George, 106
Washington, George, 88
Whiting, John W.M., 38
Wolf children, 5

Youth culture, 9, 108-109

Zeigler, Harmon, 91
Zellman, Gail L., 95